Ernest R. Suffling

Jethou - Crusoe Life in the Channel Isles

Third Edition

Ernest R. Suffling

Jethou - Crusoe Life in the Channel Isles
Third Edition

ISBN/EAN: 9783744731478

Printed in Europe, USA, Canada, Australia, Japan

Cover: Foto ©ninafisch / pixelio.de

More available books at **www.hansebooks.com**

OR

CRUSOE LIFE IN THE CHANNEL ISLES

ILLUSTRATED BY DRAWINGS PREPARED FROM AUTHOR'S OWN SKETCHES

BY

E. R. SUFFLING

*Author of "History and Legends of the Broad District,"
"How to Organize a Cruise on the Broads,"
"Afloat in a Gipsy Van," etc.*

THIRD EDITION

LONDON
JARROLD & SONS, 10 & 11, WARWICK LANE, E.C.
[*All Rights Reserved*]
1898

PREFACE.

As the writer does not pretend to possess what is termed literary style, he would ask the indulgence of the reader in any little slip of the pen which may occur in these pages, as it is not every Crusoe who can command the facile quill, the pure style, or the lively imagination of a Daniel Defoe, to narrate his adventures.

It must be borne in mind that the island of Juan Fernandez possessed many natural features, and a far greater area than Jethou can boast of, and therefore more scope for the development of incidents and descriptive embellishment.

Doubtless many of the adventures here placed before the public will appear puny beside the exploits of the original Crusoe; but it must be taken into consideration that the author does not, like Defoe's hero, revel in the impossible. At the same time it may be noted that the adventures detailed are of a sufficiently exciting kind as to be above any suspicion of dulness.

Juan Fernandez lies about four hundred miles from the nearest land, and it is therefore very difficult to imagine from whence the savages came who were about to convert Friday into a *fricassee*. The Friday of our story, y'clept Monday, came to Jethou in a natural if in an exciting manner, and it will be found that everything else in the narrative, if not an *exact* account of what really did happen, is at least feasible. It is in fact a practicable narrative, served up in a plain, ungarnished form, except that to make it more palatable to the general reader a little love-story has been introduced towards the conclusion, which, it is hoped, sustains the interest right to the last, and makes the volume end as all good books should, by allowing the principal actors to "live happily ever after."

E. R. SUFFLING (HARRY NILFORD).

Blomfield Lodge,
    Portsaown Road,
        London, W.

CONTENTS.

CHAPTER I.

My birth and home—My pretty cousin—Accident to the "Kittywich"—Journey to Guernsey—Pleading to become a Crusoe—My wish granted—Outfit secured—Sail to Jethou 9

CHAPTER II.

I take possession of the Island—Landing stores—A grand carousal—Farewell—Alone 24

CHAPTER III.

First thoughts and impressions—A tour of the Island and description 32

CHAPTER IV.

Farming operations—I make a plough and a cart—A donkey hunt—Dumb helpers—My live stock ... 44

CHAPTER V.

Canoeing—Fish of the place—The ormer and limpet—A curious fishing adventure—Queer captures from the sea—Rock fish—Construct a fish pond and water-mill 55

CHAPTER VI.

"Flapp," the gull—Surgical operation—The gull who refused to die—Taxidermy extraordinary—Feathered friends—Snakes 69

CHAPTER VII.

I build a curious "box-boat"—An unpleasant night at sea—My Sunday service—The poem, "Alexander Selkirk"—Its applicability to my lot 79

CONTENTS.

CHAPTER VIII.

A trip to St. Sampson's harbour—A horrid porcine murder—A voyage round Sark—Nearly capsized—Trip round Guernsey—The pepper-box—Curiosity of tourists ... 93

CHAPTER IX.

Harvest operations—Explore La Creux Derrible, and nearly lose my life—Crusoe on crutches—An extraordinary discovery—Kill a grampus—Oil on troubled waters—Make an overflow pump 112

CHAPTER X.

A storm and a wreck—The castaway—Dead—A night of horror—The boathouse destroyed—A burial at sea ... 126

CHAPTER XI.

Climate in Winter—Vision of my father—A warning voice—Supernatural manifestations—The falling rock—My life saved by my dog 139

CHAPTER XII.

A fairy pool—Wonders of the deep—Portrait of a poet—The cave of Fauconnaire—A letter from home and my answer to it 148

CHAPTER XIII.

Another terrible storm—Loss of the "Yellow Boy"—A ketch wrecked—I rescue a man from the sea, badly injured—He recovers 159

CHAPTER XIV.

Work and song—Sunday service—Build a larger boat, the "Anglo-Franc"—Collecting wreckage—Commence a jetty—Our cookery—Blasting operations—The opening banquet 172

CHAPTER XV.

Trawling for fish and dredging for curios—Some remarkable finds—A ghastly resurrection—The mysterious paper—The hieroglyphic—A dangerous fall—*Hors de combat*—Attempts to unravel the paper 181

CONTENTS.

CHAPTER XVI.

Yarns: The cabbages which hung their heads—The raft of spruce—Voyage of the "Dewdrop"—A lucky family—A deep, deep draught—The maire's cat 193

CHAPTER XVII.

The Will again—Searching for a clue to the paper—Barbe Rouge's Will—A probable clue—Hopes and doubts—Perplexed—A memorable trawl by moonlight—A real clue at last—The place of the skull found 207

CHAPTER XVIII.

Digging for the treasure—A noonday rest—The ghastly tenant of the treasure house—We find the treasure—An account of what we discovered 217

CHAPTER XIX.

Preparing to leave—A letter home—We lengthen and enlarge the "Anglo-Franc"—Re-christen her "Happy Return"—Love at first sight—Victualling and stowing cargo—Pretty Jeannette—The long voyage—Incidents en route—Vegetarians, and their diet—Yarmouth reached—Fresh-water navigation—My native heath ... 231

CHAPTER XX.

I surprise the old folks at home—All well—Is Priscilla false—We meet—The missing letters—A snake in the grass—Dreams of vengeance 250

CHAPTER XXI.

The "Happy Return" inspected—More of my father's ghost—Unpacking the treasure—Seek an interview with Walter Johnson—Two letters 257

CHAPTER XXII.

M. Oudin arrives—The Wedding Day—Division of the spoil—Alec returns to Jethou—Wedding gifts—The end 265

APPENDIX.

A few words about the Channel Isles 271

LIST OF ILLUSTRATIONS.

		PAGE
THE ISLAND OF JETHOU ...	*Frontispiece*	1
THE OLD HOME AT BARTON ...	... ...	10
MAP OF THE ISLAND OF JETHOU	... ...	35
PLAN OF HOMESTEAD ...	... ...	43
MY PLOUGH	... ...	47
AN ANTEDILUVIAN CHARIOT ...	... ...	48
"I WAS SWAMPED IN A MOMENT"	... ...	61
THE "YELLOW BOY," PLANS, ETC.	... ...	81
A PORCINE MURDER ...	... ...	99
ROCKS AT SOUTH END OF SARK	... ...	101
THE MAIN PATH OF THE ISLAND	... ...	113
LA CREUX DERRIBLE ...	...	119
TOO LATE!	...	131
A GHOSTLY VISITANT	... ...	141
"ALONG THE RUGGED CLIFF PATH" ...	...	161
RESCUE OF ALEC DUCAS ...	...	167
THE PUZZLING DOCUMENT	...	186, 209
A TERRIBLE FALL	... ...	187
THE TENANT OF THE TREASURE HOUSE	...	223
LENGTHENING THE "ANGLO-FRANC" ...	...	235

JETHOU;

OR,

Crusoe Life in the Channel Isles.

CHAPTER I.

MY BIRTH AND HOME—MY PRETTY COUSIN—ACCIDENT TO THE "KITTYWICH"—JOURNEY TO GUERNSEY—PLEADING TO BECOME A CRUSOE—MY WISH GRANTED—OUTFIT SECURED—SAIL TO JETHOU.

THAT Crusoe of Crusoes, Alexander Selkirk, as I am aware, commences his entertaining history with his birth and parentage, and as I am also a Crusoe, although a very minor adventurer, I may as well follow the precedent and declare my nativity.

I was born at the little village of Barton in Norfolk, at the time the guns at Balaclava were mowing down our red coats and tars, where my father had a small house facing the Broad. It was a comfortable old two-storied building, with a thatched roof, through which a couple of dormer windows peered out, like two eyes, over the beautiful green lawn which sloped to the reed-fringed water. My father was in very comfortable circumstances, as he was owner of six

THE OLD HOME AT BARTON.

large fishing vessels hailing from the port of Great Yarmouth, some ten or twelve miles distant as the crow flies.

Being born, as it were, on the water (for a distance of a hundred yards matters but little), I was naturally from my birth a young water dog, although they tell me that for some months after I made my bow to the world, milk also played a prominent part in my career.

As I grew into boyhood, of course I had my rowing punt and my rod, and thus gained my first taste for a solitary life, as it frequently happened that I would be away from sunrise to sunset on some little expedition to one or other of the neighbouring Broads. By and bye came the time when I arrived at that rare age for enjoyment, fourteen years. This birthday, the fourteenth, was a red-letter day in my life, as I received two presents, which were in my eyes very valuable ones; my uncle presented me with a beautiful little light gun, and my father handed me over his small sailing boat. Now I was a man! I felt it, and I knew it, and so did my schoolmates, for there was not one of them, who at some time or other, had not felt the effects of my prowess in a striking manner. Still, the drubbings I gave were not always to my credit, for I was a very big and strong lad for my age, and my self-imposed tasks of long rowing trips and other athletic exercises, naturally made me powerful in the arms and chest. Of my brain power I shall say little, as my mind was ever bent on sporting topics when it should have been diving into English history or vulgar fractions. Some new device in fishing gear was always of more consequence to me than any inquiry as to the name of the executioner who gave Charles the I. "chops for breakfast," as we youngsters used to say, when we irreverently spoke of the decollation of his Majesty.

Still, somehow I stumbled through my schooling

till I was sixteen, when I was sent off to my father's office on the Quay at Yarmouth to take charge of the books, which were an everlasting humdrum record of herrings and the various trawl fish which came in so frequently in our vessels.

Between whiles I had plenty of spare time, and whenever a few hours were allowed me, I could not keep out of my boat, so that if the sea happened to be fairly calm, I was sure to be found bobbing about on it, and was as well known by the fishermen along the coast ten miles north and south of Yarmouth, as I was by the folks in my own village. When the sea was rough I turned my attention to Breydon Water, or the Bure, or other of the rivers flowing into it, so that at an early age I could command my little boat as easily as one manages a horse in driving. On Saturdays, when the wind and weather were at all favourable, I used frequently to hurry away from business as early as possible, and sail home along the Bure and Ant, a distance of about twenty miles, rather more than less, and became so accustomed to the route that I knew every tree and post, aye, and almost every reed and bulrush on the river's bank on my homeward way.

Sometimes night would close in rather quickly upon me, but as I only had two turnings to look out for, Thurne Mouth and Ant Mouth, I seldom made a mistake, however dark it might be, especially when the venerable old ruined gateway of St. Benet's Abbey was once passed.

Almost always these trips were solitary ones, if I except the companionship of my retriever "Begum," who was a present from my cousin on his return from India. Begum, he informed me, was a ruler in India, but whether male or female I never discovered.

My dog was a gentleman, but to this day it has remained a matter of conjecture with me, as to whether we inadvertantly gave him a lady's name or no. Anyway, "Begum" sounded well; he was a ruler, and being black coincided with our school rulers, which were always black with ink. Unfortunately, everyone persisted (possibly to annoy me if they could), in calling him By Gum! strongly accentuating the second word, and till the poor old dog died, the name stuck to him like a postage stamp to a letter.

In my holiday trips I had a companion, my cousin Priscilla, who was, if the term be permissible, as great a water dog as myself. I am not going to attempt a description of her, but I *must* let the reader know that she was bigger, stronger, and a vast deal prettier than any girl within a radius of many miles of our village; not that I wish to disparage the looks or figures of our Norfolk girls, for they can hold their own with the rest of England, as Bad King Harry knew when he wooed and won Norfolk's Queen, Mistress Anne Boleyn of Blickling.

'Cilla, as I called my cousin for brevity, could row, sail a boat, skate, and shoot; yes, she was a very fair shot, and never a winter passed but she gave a good account of duck, teal, mallard, pewit, and geese, as the result of her prowess.

But I will say no more of pretty cousin 'Cilla at present, as this narrative is to be a record of what more nearly concerns myself, so I must not "*mardle*," as we say in Norfolk, but proceed with my story.

I was twenty-one and some months more, for the rejoicings consequent upon the event had become matter of past history, when my father one day received intelligence of one of his fishing vessels having been towed in a disabled state into the harbour of St. Peter Port, Guernsey. She was so badly damaged that his presence was imperative, to decide as to her ultimate fate.

She had been to a Spanish port for cork and hemp, as the fishing season was not a very good one, and on her return voyage had run upon an island called Jethou, during a dense fog, luckily in a calm sea, or she would never have come off whole again. Nothing ever does when it once plays at ramming these granite islands. Like the Syrens, who lured or tried to lure Ulysses, these islands are very fair to behold; but woe to the ship that comes into contact with them, for they rarely escape from their deadly embrace.

The very next day (my father having allowed me to accompany him) we started for Plymouth, a long journey, *via* London, at which city, being my first visit to the metropolis, I could fain have broken our journey, but our business being urgent we steamed away to Plymouth by the night train. After a substantial meal next morning we sallied out to find the first vessel sailing to Guernsey, and were lucky in discovering one called the "Fawn," which was preparing to sail the same day. Although only a cargo ketch the skipper bargained to take us, and about two p.m. we unmoored and were soon off. Our passage was a quick one, a strong N.W. wind bowling us over to St. Peter Port in time for early breakfast next morning.

It is needless for me to go through the whole story of the running ashore of our smack, as beyond the important fact that it was her mishap which caused me ever to visit the Channel Islands, she has little else to do with my narrative.

She was damaged very seriously amidships, but my father, who had a happy knack of turning almost everything to a good account, unless irredeemably hopeless, was struck with a capital idea in this instance. Instead of selling her as a worthless hulk, he had her cut in two, the damaged timbers removed, a new length of keel laid down, and had her lengthened about ten feet; after which operation she was as sound as ever, and as my father had prophesied, no one recognized her again for the same vessel.

While we were waiting for the "Kittywitch" (for that was her name) to be run off the slips, we had plenty of time to look about us; in fact, we spent nearly seven weeks among these lovely islands.

We explored Guernsey and Sark thoroughly, also Herm as far as we were allowed, that island being more of a proprietary place than the others. We also spent about ten days in Jersey, which is quite a large place in comparison with the other islands. But of all the islands, I think Sark carries off the palm, not that it has beauties of its own, or is grander or more prolific, but it is an *epitome* of all the other islands; in fact it contains in a small space every salient feature of the Channel Isles; the people, the granite cliffs, the bays, the caves, the hills, the woods, the shady lanes, the sandy beaches, are all there, and the surrounding sea is not a tone the less blue in its intensity, nor the air a whit less balmy than that with which the other islands are favoured.

Now it happened, while we were staying at St. Peter Port, awaiting the re-launching of our vessel, that we made friends with the proprietor of the island of Jethou, upon which the "Kittywich" struck, and although it was a good three miles from St. Peter's harbour, yet we made occasional trips to the islet when the wind was fair and the sea smooth. With this little island of Jethou I was charmed, and fancied I could make it my Paradise, if only I could be allowed to live there for a twelvemonth, *a la* Robinson Crusoe.

At this idea my father, who was a thoroughly business-like, matter-of-fact man, set up his eyes and called me a name not at all polite; but as he was my parent, and viewed life through older optics than mine, I daresay he was right in the main, when he called me, to put it mildly, a "stupid fool." But although he pooh-poohed the idea, and bade me dismiss it from my mind, I could not help the thought entering my brain, and I wished something might possibly happen by which I might be left alone on the island, to try, at all events, what Crusoe life was really like.

Sure enough something did happen which ultimately gave me the opportunity of carrying out my idea in its entirety. M. Oudin, the proprietor of the island, had two events to chronicle in one day, events which quite altered his after life, and took him at an hour's notice from his Jethou home to Gardner's Hotel, Guernsey.

A letter arrived at St. Peter Port for him, from Paris, which, according to custom, was placed in the guernsey breast of a fisherman, who sailed with it straightway to M. Oudin. The latter gentleman having adjusted his glasses, after instructing his man to give the messenger spirituous refreshment (which is so very cheap in these islands), proceeded to scan the contents of the letter. It was from a lawyer in Paris, informing him of the decease of his brother, a leather merchant, who, dying wifeless and childless, had bequeathed him both his business and fortune. This intelligence of both joy and sorrow so bewildered and unstrung the nerves of M. Oudin that, in accordance with his custom, he took a dram—in fact the circumstances were so very warrantable that he took two— and probably even more; or else they were like Mynheer Van Dunk's, "deep, *deep* draughts." Anyway, upon giving the fisherman orders to sail him back to Guernsey, and attempting to follow him with his serving man, they somehow found themselves at the bottom of the gulch which led down to the shore (upon which the boat was careened), so much mixed as to arms and legs, that an observer would have wondered what curious animal he was gazing upon. Two of them scrambled to their feet, and as well as they could, shook themselves together; but the third, M. Oudin, had unfortunately broken his right thighbone completely in two. Then the maudlin men, despite his groans, placed him awkwardly in the boat, and hoisted sail for Guernsey.

As luck would have it, my father and I were standing upon the deck of the now nearly finished "Kittywich," when the boat came in, and M. Oudin having communicated to my father the nature of his hurt, my dad immediately gave orders for him to be taken to Gardner's Hotel, where we were staying, and hurrying for a doctor soon joined him there. The leg was set, and I spent the greater part of each day by the side of M. Oudin's bed, chatting and reading to him, and attending to his wants. During our conversation I happened to mention what a great treat I should consider it to be allowed to live on his island for a few months. Presently we went more fully into the "whys and wherefores" of the case, so that I quite began to imagine it might all come to pass as I wished, but the arrival of my father in the midst of our very pleasant conversation quite put a damper on the scheme.

"Bah! he would hear nothing of it; it was a mad fool's idea. No, no, think no more of such rubbish, my boy. Crusoe is all very well to *read*, but it's a poor look out to have to *live* Crusoe."

M. Oudin, seeing how my mind was bent upon the scheme, gave my father a day or two to simmer down, and then took him in hand quietly and practically.

"Now look here, Nilford," said M. Oudin, motioning my respected father to draw his chair nearer to the bed-side, "as you know, I must for the present, at all events, leave Jethou, for by my brother's death my presence is necessary in Paris. By his decease I become possessed of a fortune of upwards of 700,000 francs and a large business to boot. Now a business employing upwards of forty men will require my constant supervision, and it is therefore very unlikely that I shall ever return to Jethou, except perhaps for a very brief holiday.

"Now, during my enforced sojourn in this town, your son has shewn me every attention and kindness, and with your permission I will give him the whole of my interest in Jethou as a reward for his attention to me during my recovery. The island is Crown property, which I rent for a nominal sum, and as to the furniture, fixtures, and live stock they shall be his (by your permission) to do as he likes with."

My father made a wry face at this, while I, who sat speechless, could feel my heart bounding against my ribs for very joy. Alas! my father negatived the whole thing. "It was not to be thought of; it could not be carried out by a youngster like me; I should perhaps die without assistance reaching me; I might starve," and a score more obstacles were mentioned. By and bye, however, with my earnest persuasion, backed up by M. Oudin's quiet but forcible manner, my dad melted so far as to ask for a couple of days for consideration.

Oh! those two days, would they never pass? Yes, they rolled by at last, and once more we were seated in M. Oudin's room.

"Well, Nilford, what is your decision? I trust it is a favourable one for the lad, for I am sure he would thoroughly enjoy the life; but if not, why in case he grew 'mammy sick,' he could return home. But the lad is of the right metal, and I'll warrant would see twelve months out without getting weary of the life.

Come now, Nilford, give me your hand, and boy let go."

By the way, my name is Harry Nilford, which I do not think I have mentioned before.

Then came a long verbal tug of war between these two good men, in which I could discern that my father's refusal was solely based upon his love for me and his apprehension for my safety. The tug of words, like a tug of war at an athletic meeting, was a long one, first one gained an advantage only to lose it to his opponent directly after; then the opponent would get in a strong verbal tug, and nearly draw his man over the line; but at length my father, with great reluctance, conceded a point, a great point in fact, one which virtually settled the contest.

"M. Oudin," said my parent, "I'll consent on one condition, which is, that I may be allowed to draw up an agreement as to the boy's tenancy of the island, and if Harry agrees to abide by it, well and good."

"Very well, father," I quickly put in, "here are writing implements; draw up your Code and I will soon tell you my decision."

This was said with great emphasis on the "*my*," and delivered with an air of—"see what a decided person *I* am."

In an hour my father had drawn up the following document:—

TERMS OF AGREEMENT FOR MY SON'S
RESIDENCE UPON JETHOU FOR 12 MONTHS.

My son Harry wishes to live the life of a Crusoe or Hermit, on the Island of Jethou for twelve months, and to this I agree

only on his signifying his willingness to abide by the terms stated in this agreement.
1. He shall allow no one to land on the island.
2. Shall not himself land upon any of the surrounding islands (rocks which are uninhabited excepted).
3. Shall not speak to a living soul during the course of his self-exilement.
4. Shall obtain no stores nor goods of any kind from any other island, nor from any passing vessel.
5. Shall hold no communication with anyone, in any way :—
    (*a*) Either ashore or afloat.
    (*b*) Except in case of sickness, accident, detrimental to limb or life, or
    (*c*) In other case of dire necessity.

Should my son choose to abide by the above regulations, I will agree to his holding the island for a period of one year.

Signed, THOMAS J. NILFORD.

"There!" said my father, laying down his pen, "that is my ultimatum, my son ; and mark me, I will agree to *nothing* else."

This was said in a manner which shewed plainly that he considered he had drawn up a code so stringent that he did not deem it at all likely I should accept his plan ; but to his great chagrin, and I may almost say his consternation, I reached out my hand, after reading the document, and taking the goose quill, wrote under the last clause,

"Accepted—Harry Nilford."

That being done, my father could not go back upon his word, and accordingly the whole thing was settled.

M. Oudin was pleased, and I was supremely delighted, but my good old father was quite dejected, and frankly avowed that it was like sentencing me to twelve months' imprisonment. So it was, but what a delightful imprisonment I anticipated it would be!

However, in a day or two he came round, and as he could not well alter the turn circumstances had taken, he endeavoured to ameliorate them. He made me write down a list of what I thought I should require, and to this list he added a long supplement; and after mature consultation with M. Oudin, another list was added as as addendum; in fact, the articles were so numerous that they filled four huge packing cases.

These cases were zinc-lined to keep the goods dry, as some of them were perishable, and no one can tell with what pride I gazed at these boxes, and thought of the glorious life I was about to lead. No thought of any accident, or other drawback, even entered my head; in fact, as I sat on the top of a case, swinging my legs and counting the hours which had to pass before the day arrived when I was to take possession of my island home, I was most consummately happy, being naturally ignorant of what was to befall me.

At length came the day for launching the "Kittywich," at which I assisted to my utmost; for I knew that any hitch with her meant further detention in Guernsey for me. All went well, and as she slid off the stocks (like a duck entering the water) without a splash or jar of any kind, a ringing cheer went up, and then I knew that I should soon bid farewell to picturesque St. Peter Port, one of the finest harbour towns of Great Britain.

A few more days and the "Kittywich" had received

her cargo for home, and with it a new name, for in consideration of her additional carrying capacity, we rechristened her the "Cormorant." Then came the day on which the Blue Peter was seen at her masthead, but what was even better in my eyes, was my own outfit packed in the four huge cases which stood so prominently on her hatchway amidships.

M. Oudin hobbled down to the harbour to see us off, and in doing so handed me a long heavy case as a parting gift, with instructions not to open it for a week, by which time he hoped to be far away in Paris.

We unmoored, left the harbour, and in an hour were laying at anchor off the north end of Jethou.

CHAPTER II.

I TAKE POSSESSION OF THE ISLAND—LANDING STORES — A GRAND CAROUSAL — FAREWELL— ALONE.

THE 2nd March, 187—, was a bright mild day, with but little wind and a quiet sea: just the day for landing my stores. The goods I had selected, and those added by my father and M. Oudin, were of a very miscellaneous kind, and included provisions, farm and garden seeds (and a few implements), a canoe, a gun, clothing, fishing gear, oil and coal, cooking apparatus, and a score other things. As I knew the island was devoid of animals except rabbits, I asked for, and obtained some live stock—in fact, quite a farmyard. There were a goat, a dog, a cat, six pigeons, two pigs, six fowls, and last, though by no means least, a young donkey.

The large cases of goods were landed in a boat, not without a slight mishap, however, as one of them, in being lowered over the bulwarks, was carelessly unhitched by the men in the boat and tumbled overboard; it fell in three fathoms of water, but the water was so translucent that it was clearly discernible on the bottom.

This took quite an hour to get up, as it was an awkward thing to grapple, but there were plenty of hands willing to help in landing the goods, as several of the Guernsey men had come over to have a parting spree.

The pigs and donkey were pushed overboard and quickly reached the shore; the former, in spite of popular belief, proving themselves excellent swimmers when once they struck out shorewards, especially as the distance was short. On landing they went up over the island, and for the time disappeared among the rocks and wild bushes.

By dusk the cry was, "All ashore," as everything had been landed, and the "Cormorant" brought to a safe mooring under the lee of the rocky island of Creviçon.

Altogether there were nearly twenty of us, that is, my father and self, the skipper and crew of the "Kitty," and several of the workmen who had been employed in altering and repairing the vessel; also the master shipwright, in whose charge the vessel had been.

First came a grand spread in the principal room of the house, the provisions for which had been brought over from St. Peter Port. It was a great success, and after the improvised table had been cleared away (boxes, surmounted by planks covered with a sail, formed the table) the fun commenced. Joke followed joke, and song followed song. Then came toasts and sentiments, which were of quite an international character, as songs and sentiments in English, French, and Spanish were continuously fired off, most of them being of a seafaring character.

The skipper of the "Cormorant" led off with a regular old North Sea song, called, "The Dark-eyed Sailor." It is probably known by nearly every seaman in the North Sea Fishery, and is a great favourite at all carousals. It commences:

> " It's of a comely young maiden fair,
> Who walked on the quay to take the air,
> She met a young sailor on the way,
> So I paid attention, so I paid attention to what they did say."

This song, sung by a Norfolk man, always seems to me a great curiosity, as the last line is lengthened out and twisted about in a most grotesque manner, apparently to suit the whim or fancy of the singer, for no two of them seem to conjure vocally with it in the same way. Everyone present is supposed to join in the last line as a kind of chorus, and not only join in, but "give it lungs," as they say. Some of them pay such attention to these points, that they appear in danger of lockjaw, or the starting of a blood-vessel, so heartily do they sing.

Then came a French song, with a chorus something about " Houp, houp, houp à tra-la-la-la !" the singer standing on the top of an empty barrel to warble, and as he set the fashion, so every succeeding singer followed suit, and mounted the "pulpit," as they dubbed the cask.

Old Roscoe, our wooden-legged mate (the right leg of flesh having been lost in my father's service), gave a funny jaw-breaking Scotch song, with a chorus which no one could repeat, so when the chorus came he sang it alone, while we contented ourselves with howling "Rule Britannia"—at least all those who knew it, while the others who did not, laughed and smoked.

Then a Spaniard (who was a shipwright) sang one of his national songs to an accompaniment of thumb-snapping (to imitate castanets), at which he was very expert. He had a fine baritone voice, and his song was full of fire, being a famous bull-fighting ditty, in which El Toro came in for a dashing chorus.

By and bye the fun became still faster and more furious, till old Ross, of the timber-toe, took exception and would insist on order being kept. Ross always constituted himself Master of the Ceremonies when anything festive was on foot, and our men, as a matter of course, left everything in his hands; but the men of St. Peter Port knew him not, and would have no authority from him, and as a kind of good-natured revenge for his interference, some of them played a practical joke upon him; but they did not know their man, for no sooner had the joke been carried into effect (gunpowder in his pipe) than Ross seized his stick and knocked two of his tormentors down, the rest quickly fleeing out of doors. His wooden leg greatly handicapped him, but he at length got one of the men in a corner, who, on finding there was no means of escape, struck out right and left at Ross's somewhat prominent nose, causing the claret to flow like the cataract of Lodore. Now his Scotch blood was up, and he certainly would have done his assailant an injury, as he was a very powerful man, had not some of his comrades rescued him. But this did not appease his fury, for he went at them all with a glass bottle in one hand and a heavy stick in the other; but luckily his career was cut short by a man who ran behind him, and with a well-directed blow with an iron rod broke his leg clean in two just below the knee—the wooden one, of course. Down came the hero, who in his rage tore up the earth around him to fling at the circle of grinning faces. By this time my father and the skipper came upon the scene, and after a time cooled down the gallant Scot, and persuaded him to "gang awa" to bed, which he did, going in state, borne at the *four* corners by four of his shipmates.

This incident put a stop to the singing, but commenced fun in another way. Some of the fellows cut up the remains of Ross's leg and stick and set them on fire, the barrel which had done duty for a rostrum being also broken up and added; other wooden articles were quickly flung on, till at length quite a large bonfire was formed, round which these excited men danced hand-in-hand like children round a Maypole. Their manners, however, were hardly childlike, for they jumped, and yelled, and sang with the ruddy firelight glowing on their countenances, till they looked like a lot of demons performing some diabolical incantation. All around was the dark night, and rocks, and trees, which gave a most weird aspect to the scene when viewed from a short distance.

And thus they were enjoying their pandemonium when my father, the skipper, and I left them in the "wee sma' hours" and retired to rest.

* * *

How long they kept it up I know not, but when I awoke and dressed at daylight all was quiet. At six all hands were called, and a sorry sight they presented. Ross had mounted a jury-leg, while among the other men no less than three black eyes appeared, beside bruised cheeks, and red swollen noses. However, all were friendly again, and agreed that they had hardly ever before spent such a jolly night. Such was a sailor's idea of a jolly time or "high old spree!"

Breakfast over, my goods were hauled from the beach and placed in the different rooms and sheds according to their kind, while by noon the "Cormorant," with her Blue Peter flying, was ready for a start northward to dear old England. The Guernseaise had departed amid give and take cheering directly after breakfast, so that only the crew of the vessel remained. My father bade me an affectionate farewell on the deck of the vessel, but at the last embrace I felt too full of emotion to speak, for a lump was in my throat, and a tear started from my father's eye and rolled down his bronzed cheek, so that I knew that he, too, was greatly moved at losing me for such a long period. A firm grip of the hand told without words how we, father and son, loved each other, and to hide my emotion I tumbled over the bulwarks into the dingy, and was pulled ashore by a couple of hands, amid the hearty cheers of the men who stood on deck. They gave me a salute of twelve *guns* (fired from two revolvers).

I stood on the rocky shore and waved a tablecloth tied to a boat-hook till the vessel was hull down on the horizon, and then turned my face to my island home, not feeling nearly so happy as I had anticipated a month before. Alone! I felt as if the whole world had departed from me, and that I was the sole survivor of the human race.

CHAPTER III.

FIRST THOUGHTS AND IMPRESSIONS—A TOUR OF THE ISLAND AND DESCRIPTION.

AS I walked up the rocky path leading to the house, I must confess I felt anything but sprightly. I felt that Crusoe life, after all, was not all *caviare*. I was very depressed, and must admit a few tears, as the whole force of what I had undertaken presented itself vividly to my mind. What if I met with an accident? What if I were taken ill? Suppose someone put in at night and cut my throat for the sake of plunder? Who would help me? Who would know of my position? Might I not die any one of a hundred deaths without the fact being known for weeks, perhaps months? What did this idiotic idea of mine amount to after all? Where was the pleasure? Would it not be better to be home in dear old Barton with my skiff and pretty Priscilla?

Such were some of my thoughts, but my depression I cannot so readily sprinkle on paper, and will not try to describe it. Let it suffice that *I was* depressed, and deeply too.

I felt thirsty, so wandered to the house and sat down and poured myself out a bottle of Bass, and as I drank it, became aware of the presence of my dog, who placed his muzzle in my hand and looked into my face with positively tears in his dear old eyes. Why, after all, I was not alone. No, here was a friend indeed (teste Byron), who would be ever by my side in weal and woe. "Poor dog, are you hungry then?" Yes he was, and by the bye, why should I not try something? We ate; and in half an hour—such is the changeableness of the human mind—I was as happy as a sand-boy (whatever that may be), as I wandered by the sunny shore.

I would make a tour of inspection of my estate; and, reader, if you will kindly accompany me, I will show you the different sights of my little island.

Jethou, I must premise, is about half a mile long by a quarter wide. It rises steeply from the sea all round, except at the North end, where the slope is somewhat gentle. It is a dome-shaped mass, rising at the summit to a height of nearly three hundred feet. It may serve to give a good idea of its form if I liken it to a huge dish cover (a Britannia metal one, if you will, for it is crown property), as it is very symmetrical when viewed from a distance. It is, in fact, a huge bosom-like hill, around which three paths are cut; the first varying from fifty to a hundred feet above the sea, the second averages one hundred and fifty feet above high water, and another runs round perhaps fifty feet higher still. These paths at certain points are connected by other paths, so that one may readily get from one elevation to another, except where the island is unusually steep, when zig-zag paths have to be negotiated. In one part seven or eight zig-zags have to be walked to rise to an elevation of about sixty or seventy feet, so steep is the south end of the island. At the north-west rises a curious pyramidal mass of granite, about one hundred and twenty feet above high water, called Creviçon, which may be reached on foot at low tide or even quarter flood; but after the tide once gets above the boulders it comes in like a mill race, rising at times during certain winds as much as seven feet within the hour; so that one may be cut off from the main island in a very few minutes, as it would be madness to try and cross during a heavy sea, whatever excellent swimming powers one might possess, as the rush of the tide would sweep one away like a straw.

Strange to say, there is another of these vast piles of granite, but of greater altitude and bulk, at the south end of the island, with just such a race of water running between it and the mainland after the tide turns. It is called La Fauconnaire, or the Falconry, and approaches two hundred feet in height, and very difficult of ascent. Each of these rock-islands is surmounted by a stone beacon in form of a miniature lighthouse tower (without the lantern story), about fifteen feet high. These beacons serve seamen as landmarks from which to take bearings, and to warn them of the danger of a too near approach to this dreadful coast—or rather coasts—for all these islands are terrible places in rough weather.

Now I will ask the reader to accompany me on a brief tour round the island. Starting from the house,

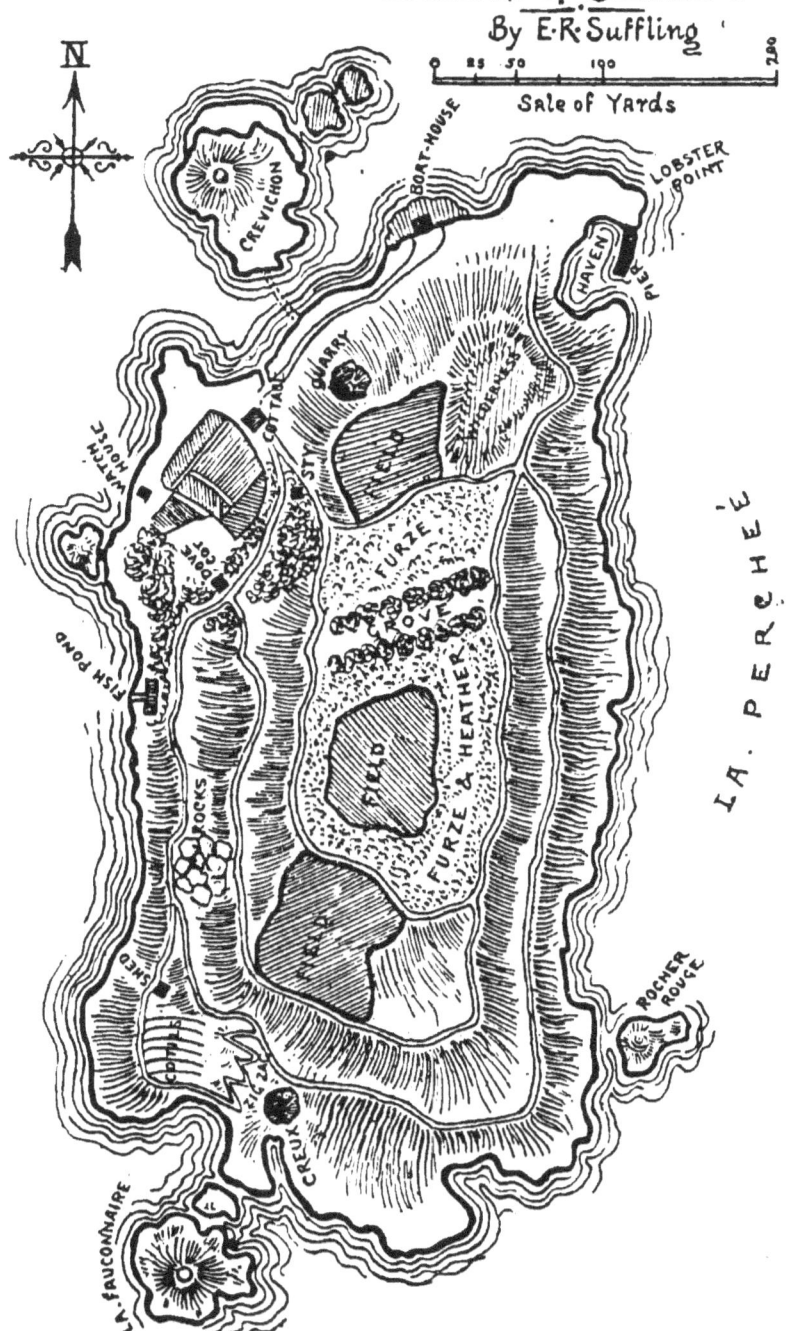

past the pigeon-tower, we pass under some large walnut trees so thickly planted as to make the part very shady, even on a bright day, and on dull days quite gloomy. We take the middle path, which is about four feet wide, and flanked on each side by braken and boulders. Indeed, nearly half the island consists of brakes and granite blocks. I will mention the various items of interest as we pass along, if the reader will supply his own imaginings of whirling seagulls, frisking rabbits, sea breezes, bellowing surge as it bumps and breaks against the granite sides of the island, flowers and bloom, singing birds and sweet-smelling shrubs, etc. These things a mere pen, however facile and graceful, cannot adequately describe without the help of the reader's brain; so I will ask him to imagine the above for himself, but I must warn him not to take cold with his lively imagination, as occasionally the March winds are very keen here, and in the present age of hypnotism, and thought-reading, and like gymnastics of the brain, it is very easy to make the imagination play pranks of an undesirable nature.

Now to resume our walk. Taking the middle path we quickly ascend to a height of nearly two hundred feet above the boiling surge dashing against the impregnable rocks below, and get a splendid view of Guernsey, a good three miles distant, stretching far away to the north, where it lies so low that it seems to melt gradually away into the sea. Presently we come to some huge rocks which lie so much in our path that the footway has to wind round them. They are huge masses of granite so poised that apparently a good push would send them rolling into the sea below, but their very size makes them secure, as some of the larger ones must certainly weigh forty or fifty tons, and the wind would have to blow a hurricane indeed which would dislodge them.

Here is one weighing perhaps three or four hundredweight which I will try and push over. I tug, and push, and presently it nods, and nods, and rolls over and over, till gathering impetus down the steep side of the island, it crashes with irresistible force through the furze, and heather, and shrubs, clearing a path as it goes till it reaches the granite rocks, upon which it crashes and bounds, breaking off great splinters, till finally with a boom it buries itself in the foam, never more to be seen by mortal eyes.

Following the path we come to some curious terraces, one above the other, which form a hanging garden facing due south. Now covered with turf, it was many years ago a famous potato garden. This spot is known as the Cotils.

Almost opposite this end of the island and at a short distance, rises the huge pyramidal mass of granite called La Fauconnaire (The Falconry). It is nearly two hundred feet high, and surmounted, as already mentioned, by a white stone beacon, which from Jethou looks the shape and size of a loaf of white sugar; but a scramble to the top of the rocks for those who have nerve to climb the steep sides of La Fauconnaire, will show that the sugar loaf is fifteen feet high. La Fauconnaire is, I believe, unclimbable except at one place, at least for those who are not experienced cragsmen or Alpine experts. At low water a causeway of rocks joins it to the mainland, but at half-tide even it is impassable, except in a boat on a calm day. On a windy day such a strong tide rushes through the strait that a boat would be swept away in the attempt to cross, although the distance is only four or five hundred feet. The narrowness of the channel makes the rush greater.

Still keeping the middle path we come to an awful yawning chasm in the earth, called La Creux Terrible. Its sides are so sheer that one shudders to approach its crumbling brink for fear a slip should mean a step into eternity. No man could fall here and live to tell the sensation. Standing near the brink one can just discern the bottom, and hear the sea surging and rolling along the floor as the tide gradually rises. The chasm is funnel-shaped, and about two hundred feet deep by about one hundred feet across. The bottom is connected with the beach by a cavern, which may be entered at low tide, and the view taken from below upward; but woe to the individual caught in this cave, for he would have but a poor chance for his life if the tide once hemmed him in.

Leaving this dreadful place, which I never approached but twice in the dark, we shortly come to a very noticeable rock rising from the sea; it is called Le Rocher Rouge, but as the apex takes the form of a gigantic arm-chair, I have taken the liberty (as I have done with many other places and things) of re-christening it Trône de Neptune (Neptune's Throne), and it has so fixed itself in my mind, that I have often during a stormy night wondered if he might not be sitting there ruling the elements, but never had the temerity to go and see. I may here tell the reader that although not naturally superstitious, I have a way of peopling my island with beings during the solitary walks I take in the day, that at night I almost fancy these spirit-forms hover round me—perhaps watching me. It may be that I have mistaken the flight of a sea-gull or night-bird for something superhuman, but on several occasions I have been warned of approaching danger by something outside myself; not tangible to the touch, nor definable to the eye, but still noticeable to the ear and to the mind. Put it down a bird, as your opinion, reader, and enjoy that opinion, and let me enjoy my warning watchers, whether fowl or spirit. Perhaps during my narrative I may have more to say of my "hovering ones."

From the island, at the point opposite Neptune's Throne, a good view of Sark is obtained; on one day it will be seen standing clearly above the sea, with Brechou or Merchant's Island clearly discernible, and La Coupée (the isthmus which holds the two parts of the island together) plainly in view in the sunlight; while on another day but a misty view of it may be obtained; on yet another day it will be quite invisible, although the distance is only about six miles.

Resuming our path, Herm is close on our right, the swift channel, La Percée, running between us and it, and as it lies in the sun looks a very beautiful picture, especially as the prettiest end, the south, is presented to our view. A little further we turn up the hill and come to a grove of rather stunted trees, standing like a double row of soldiers up to their knees in braken. It is a lovely spot, as the pretty fern-like brakes grow in great luxuriance beneath the spreading arms of the walnut and other trees. These brakes grow so tall and thick that it is quite difficult to force a passage through them, except where I have cut a narrow path leading to a clearing, across which, on hot days, I frequently swing my hammock, so as to obtain the full benefit of the cool sea breeze as I sway beneath the welcome shadow of the biggest walnut.

Beyond the grove, at the summit of the island, is my arable land, my farm, lying in a fence of wire-netting, without which I should not be able to preserve a blade of anything eatable from the hordes of rabbits which make the island a perfect warren.

We descend again to the pathway with care, as the island's side is so steep here that a trip over a stone or root might result in fatal consequences.

As we approach the north-east corner of the island we find the pathway gradually descending, till we are not more than twenty or thirty feet above sea level, and notice that a spur of land hooks out into the sea, forming quite a little bay, very rugged, and very rocky, but still very convenient as a haven in light weather. Here I keep my crab and lobster pots, as it is easily accessible from the house. I call it Baie de Homard (Lobster Bay).

Keeping along the shore, to the north end of the island, we arrive at a two-storied stone building which stands on the beach. This is my store-house (for fishing gear, etc.) and workshop, and is situated only a short distance from the house—perhaps three hundred yards. In the days of the old privateers this house played an important part, for it was fitted as a blacksmith's and carpenter's shop, and was probably a very handy place for slight repairs to be carried out at very short notice.

Leaving the Store, a beautiful velvety path, broad enough for a cart road, leads up a slight ascent skirting the beach to the house and cottage, which I naturally call by a word very dear to me in my solitude—*home*.

I will ask the reader to glance at the accompanying plan to aid him in getting a clearer idea of this homestead than my pen, unaided by pictorial effort, would convey.

A, then, is a comfortable and picturesque four-roomed cottage. B is the stable for my noble steed, Edward. C is the store-house, with loft over for straw, etc., for said noble quadruped. In the store I keep my utensils and implements for farm work, potatoes, flour, coals, and other heavy goods. D, sheltered garden for winter crops; F, the vegetable and fruit garden, in the midst of which stands an immense and very prolific mulberry tree; it spreads its branches fifty-four feet from north to south, and fifty-one feet from east to west. The garden contains fruit trees of all kinds. E, the Seigneurie or Government House —my palace—or, in plain words, a solid stone-built four-roomed house that might stand a siege. The front windows look out over the lawn, G, to the sea beyond, and those at the back command the well-walled-in fruit garden, F. H is devoted to shrubs and medicinal herbs. J is the flower-garden with a summer-house in the corner. K, the well of excellent water. L, flight of stone steps to the lower path leading round the island. M, pigeon-tower and fowl-house amidst walnut trees. N, Plantation and forest trees. O, watch house, once used as a strong room or prison. P, an old iron gun (mounted on a stone platform, which would probably fall to pieces at the first discharge) for summoning aid in case of sickness or distress. Q, road to fishing-store and boathouse. R, path up the hill to the piggery.

I think the reader may, from the foregoing, form some idea of the island and homestead, as I have taken him all round the former, and pointed out, although very briefly, the various portions of the latter. I have wasted no time nor ink in so doing, as he like myself, will doubtless find more pleasure in the narrative which commences in the succeeding chapter. A fair idea of the island is necessary, so as clearly to understand some of the incidents which are placed before the reader, and I trust I have said sufficient to enable him to follow me in what I have to tell of my sojourn on the pretty, though solitary island of Jethou.

A glance at the accompanying map will give a good idea of the various places in Jethou mentioned in this story.

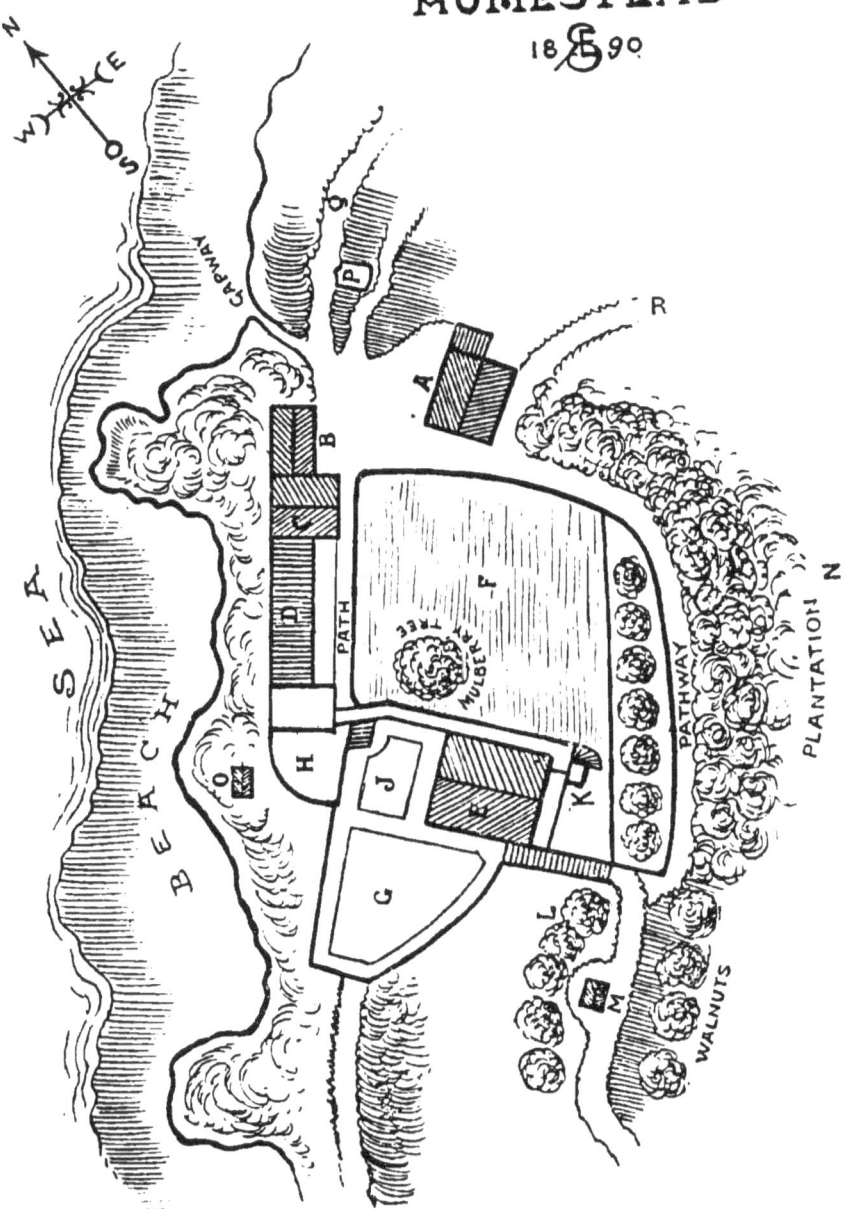

CHAPTER IV.

FARMING OPERATIONS—I MAKE A PLOUGH AND A CART—A DONKEY HUNT—DUMB HELPERS—MY LIVE STOCK.

MY first few days were spent pleasantly enough, but as soon as the sun had set my spirits would droop, and I felt anything but jolly, but like Mark Tapley, I firmly made up my mind to be happy under all circumstances.

I had a deal of unpacking to do, and determined, as my stay was to be a lengthy one, "to find a place for everything, and keep everything in its place." My initial motto was a good one, and I worked for quite a week scheming and contriving all kinds of receptacles and appliances for my heterogeneous goods and chattels.

My goat and donkey I turned loose, and as for my pigs, I had not seen them since I landed; but I trusted that they were not like the evil-tempered swine of the Bible, who cast themselves headlong into the sea, for if that were the case they could commence their suicide at any moment by rolling down any of the steep sides of the island into the sea. I trusted that my pigs were sweet-tempered beasts, and of a non-suicidal variety, and so they afterwards proved, and toothsome into the bargain.

The boathouse received my canoe, fishing gear, carpenter's tools, and gunpowder, for I was afraid to keep the latter near the house, as I had a large quantity, nearly half a hundredweight. I had this large quantity for several reasons, the principal being that I wished to shoot a large collection of sea fowl, and still have plenty for the big cannon which was to summon aid from Herm or Guernsey, should it be required. My good father had made arrangements for me to signal as follows:

If I fired a single gun, the coastguard from Herm would put off to my aid; if two guns were fired, help was to be considered very urgent, and either the coastguard or one of the peasants of Herm would put over, if the weather were calm enough to allow of a boat being launched. If I fired minute guns, either by night or day, they would be reported to the harbour master of St. Peter Port, who had my father's instructions to send out a doctor immediately. Thus I felt comparatively easy in my mind as to help in case of great need, either by accident or sickness. My gunpowder was therefore kept in the lower floor of the boathouse, as I thought it the safest place. I took only a pound at a time to the house for shooting purposes.

Having got everything stowed away to my satisfaction, my next step was to look over the island and see how I could employ my time in cultivating the soil. Near the top I found a large patch of arable land fenced in with wire netting, but it was greatly overgrown, having apparently been some time out of cultivation. I stepped it out in as correct yards as I could command by striding, and to my dismay found there were just two acres, which discovery somewhat nonplussed me for a time; for to dig over two acres with a spade was no light task, and I took time to reflect and see if I could not concoct some easier means of turning the soil than by digging.

Down I sat upon a stone and lighted my pipe—the solitary man's comforter—and with my gun across my knees ready for a stray shot, I made out my plan of campaign, after much cogitation. Why not make a plough? Nothing is made of nothing! What had I to turn into a plough? Then the idea of a real Saxon plough came into my head, and there the idea took tangible form, as I saw close by me a tree which would answer my purpose. Down went my gun, and away I trotted down the rocky path to the house, and quickly returned with an axe. I was quite out of breath when I regained the tree, having made as much haste as if the tree were provided with means of locomotion, or as if I had to cut down the tree in a given time; but that is just my way, I am much too impulsive.

A few strokes laid the tree low, and I soon had it trimmed ready for my purpose. My next care was to make a pair of wheels, and this took me much longer. I had noticed during one of my walks a large tree that had been felled for some purpose, but never used, and to it I repaired with a saw and worked away for several hours, cutting two slices from the fairly symmetrical bole, about four inches wide. These gave me a pair of solid wheels about twenty inches in diameter, which were large enough for my purpose. These I attached to a short axle and bolted to the tree which I felled, and by horizontally thrusting an iron rod, two feet long, through the nose of my plough, about eighteen inches from the end, I had my implement complete. The iron rod was to keep the pointed end of my oak tree from burying itself too deeply in the ground. It was not a beautiful object, but its usefulness condoned its ugliness.

MY PLOUGH.—UTILITY, NOT BEAUTY.

I placed my handiwork aside for a season, and the next two days made myself a curious sideless cart, which I could not help thinking bore a great resemblance to a ladder on wheels. Two more sections from the big tree formed the wheels, while a square piece of quartering thrust through formed an axletree. The shafts and body of my vehicle were two thick ash saplings twelve feet long, joined together with barrel staves two and a half feet long, with the convex sides downward; then fore and aft of the wheels I erected a species of gibbet to prevent my load from shifting, which having done, my antediluvian chariot was complete.

AN ANTEDILUVIAN CHARIOT.

Having provided my implements I now proceeded to till my land. I took a whole back-aching day to pluck all the large weeds and stones off my farm, and retired weary at night to dream of my flourishing crops of the future.

Up with the lark next morning, I set out to find my noble long-eared steed, Edward; but although I roamed about for an hour and a half I could not discover him anywhere, so breakfasted and searched again, but to no purpose. I gave him up as having been drowned whilst browsing on the toothsome but truculent thistle or gorse. I looked at my plough and cart in dismay, saying, "Man proposes, and an ass disposes." But shortly after this dismal reflection, judge of my joy when I heard his musical voice lifted up in sweet song, and borne to my enraptured ears on the balmy noontide breeze. Laugh not, reader, for the poor brute's voice *was* sweeter to me in my loneliness than that of the greatest operatic singer who ever trilled her wondrous notes.

Even after hearing the ass's braying I was a long time before I came upon him quite down upon the stony shore, with not a blade of grass nor even a thistle for for him to nibble at. How he got there is to me a problem to this day; but how I laboured to get him up again will ever remain in my mind, for it makes me feel sore all over to think of it.

Where I found him was at the south end of the island, facing rocky Fauconnaire. How I wandered up and down seeking a place for him to regain the lower path of the island. But all in vain. No place could I find; and all the afternoon I worked like a Titan, getting him up to the pathway again. Poor fellow! he was very docile, and I had thoughts of trying to carry him up; but although I got under him and lifted him, I could not climb with him, so at last had recourse to a block and fall, and after bruising and battering the poor creature somewhat, I got him to a safe ledge of rock, from whence by pushing, and tugging, and lifting, I got him up, foot after foot, till the perspiration streamed down my face. The real Robinson Crusoe never had anything half so difficult as this to contend with, and yet here was I at the outset working harder than a galley slave! I envied Robinson Crusoe number one, and went at my donkey again, till towards evening I got him to the lower path, and after a rest rode him home in triumph, lecturing him severely all the way "not to be such an ass again."

Next day I was *not* up with the lark—in fact it was

past nine before I opened my eyes, so much had the previous day's exertions tired me. I felt tired and stiff all over, but my morning tub and breakfast quickly restored me nearly to par.

Edward was now domiciled in the stable, so putting on his collar and a pair of home-made traces I harnessed him, with the help of various contrivances of cord and staples, to my mediæval cart, and *bumped* (for my cart was springless) down to the beach to gather seaweed. All day long we worked, "Eddy" and I, taking load after load to the top of the island; and the next day too was occupied in carting up seaweed or "vraic," as the natives call it, except that we also took up two or three loads of withered bracken, leaves, and other rubbish, which I burned and spread over the land.

After the ash and seaweed were spread I ploughed it in after a fashion, streaking long shallow trenches with my pointed wooden plough, till I had gone over the whole of the land. I looked at the tumbled ground with no great satisfaction, for as much of the manure-seaweed was upon the surface as under, so I turned to and ploughed crossways, which gave it a little better appearance. Then I allowed it a week to rest, taking my spade in the meantime and breaking the lumps and digging in the straying "vraic." At length I had my land in tolerable order, although the seaweed refused to rot as quickly as I desired. I reckoned, however, that it would rot in time, and thus nourish the seed I put in, and so it did.

I will not weary the readers with too much of my farming cares, but have written a little about it to show what obstacles a Crusoe has to overcome, and how hard he has to work to gain his ends. He has no one to pat his back when he is triumphant, nor anyone to sympathise with him over a failure. He is his own critic and censor. Suffice it to say that in due course I had patches of barley, clover, lucerne, mangold, carrots, etc., sown, and when once the seeds were in I had plenty of leisure for other pursuits.

Although early spring, the weather was very mild to what I had been used to on the Norfolk coast; in fact the temperature was as warm in April as it is in the East of England at the end of May.

The garden by the house also had my care, for I planted enough edibles in it to have maintained a large family, instead of a solitary being like myself. Still, I counted my animals as my family, and got to love them all, even to the little pigs. I named them all. There was my dog "Begum," the donkey "Eddy," the goat "Unicorn," which I contracted to "Corny." This name was derived from the fact that she had broken off one horn close to her head. The pigs being twins were "Romulus" and "Remus," and, like the first Romans of that name, had frequent family quarrels, which were, however, soon ended, the brothers rolling over each other in delight in their pig stye.

"Corny" gave me about a pint to a pint and a half of milk a day, which I found quite sufficient for my wants, as I only used it for breakfast and tea, water forming my invariable drink for dinner. Breakfast and tea-supper I usually took with some show of punctuality, but my dinner was eaten in all sorts of places—on the Creviçon, in my canoe, on the beach, or in the grove—in fact, just where I happened to be when I felt hungry and had my wallet with me.

"Begum" always took his meals with me, except when I was on the sea, when the poor fellow would follow my canoe round the island, and watch till I came back again. Then his joy knew no bounds. He would go fairly mad with delight, and I must confess I used to look for my comrade as fondly as if he were a brother awaiting my landing. He would carry quite a big load for me up the rocky cliff path, and esteem it quite a pleasure; but when I had anything extra heavy to take up I made him fetch "Eddy" to my aid. Strange as it may seem, this was a very simple proceeding, for I taught him in a couple of days, thus :

On the stable door I fastened a piece of wood to act as a fall-latch, which worked so easily that "Begum" could lift it with his nose and allow the door to swing open. Then "Eddy" would march out, and wherever I happened to be, would trot to me at the sound of my voice. Indeed, at length he used to follow "Begum," directly he was released, to any part of the island. Therefore, if I required "Eddy's" services when I was quite at the south end of the island, I had only to send "Begum" to fetch him, and away they would come together. This proceeding had only one drawback, and that was, that "Eddy" would always help himself to a mouthful of anything in the way of green food, which happened to be growing within his reach, if he had to come near my little farm. I verily believe that "Begum" used to take his friend past my crops on purpose, although it was by no means the easiest way to get to the Cotils, where my potato crop grew, and where I often used to go to get a shot at the sea fowl on the Fauconnaire. As the crops were principally for his own winter maintenance, I could not grudge him a bite of his food in advance.

Many a time when I have landed from my boat very tired, after a long cruise or fishing expedition, I have always found "Begum" waiting for me, ready to fetch "Eddy," at my word, to help to beach the boat and carry my gear up the cliff. This used to be of such frequent occurrence that upon the end of the boat's painter I worked a kind of collar for "Eddy" to pull upon in comfort. This collar I made of old sacking sewed over with sennet, and I must say it was quite a success, for he would hold his head out as naturally to receive the collar as a beggar would hold out his hat for the reception of an alms.

The pigeons I brought with me and placed in the cote or tower soon departed or died; possibly they were killed by hawks or other birds, but that I never could discover. Anyway, the tower was not long tenantless, for a pair of owls took up their abode there, and soon had a family of six fluffy little fellows. Instead of destroying these birds as many persons do in England, I allowed them to haunt the tower, in return for which they kept the mice down, and I could not find that they did me any kind of damage. I got quite to like their "to-whitting" and "to-wooing" more than the monotonous "cooing" of the pigeons which never did sound like music to my ears.

My six hens and a cockerel were located in the watch-house, from whence they had the run of a large piece of wild ground overhanging the cliff. Eggs I had in abundance, and even to spare, and before I left the island had over thirty fowls. Beside the fowls' eggs I could, in the spring, gather the eggs of the wild fowl inhabiting the islands by the score.

Enough of animals and birds; let us open another chapter on another topic.

CHAPTER V.

CANOEING—FISH OF THE PLACE—THE ORMER AND
LIMPET—A CURIOUS FISHING ADVENTURE—
QUEER CAPTURES FROM THE SEA—ROCK FISH
—CONSTRUCT A FISH-POND AND WATER-MILL.

WHEN the warm days and calm seas of May came I turned my thoughts to the sea, of which I am passionately fond, and of which one never seemed to tire, as one does of tame river water. Unfortunately my only vessel was a canoe about fourteen feet long by three feet beam, and for sea work, such as one gets round the shores of these islands, quite unfitted; but there it was, and I had simply Hobson's choice—that or none.

On a calm sea, with a tide running only one way, such as one gets on the English coast, the canoe was all very well and fairly safe; but here, through the Percée, as the channel is called between Herm and Jethou, the tide at times runs with great speed, and meeting with the resistance of the Ferriers and other huge rocks, whirls, and turns, and foams in all directions, so that a frail craft like a canoe would be a death-trap to anyone foolhardy enough to venture out in it. That being the case, I could only follow my canoeing hobby when the sea was calm, but even then did not venture far from land.

I had several narrow escapes from upsetting, and at last, whilst lying sleeplessly in bed (where, by-the-bye, most of my thinking and scheming is done), the idea of making alterations in my canoe came under my consideration, and before I went to sleep that night I had made up my mind to improve her stability in several ways. I would make her fore and aft compartments air-tight, so that if she turned turtle she would act as a life preserver, and moreover, why not add an outrigger, such as the natives of the Pacific have to theirs, making them almost impossible to upset?

The second day saw my plans an accomplished fact. I put in bulkheads fore and aft, and pitched the canoe inside and out, making her heavier, but thoroughly water-tight—the end compartments being even air-tight. I raised the combing of the well to six inches in height, put on a deeper keel, shortened my mast, and added an outrigger. What more *could* I do? The outrigger I made of a bundle of bamboos lashed firmly together, like the pictures one sees of the old Roman Fascines, or Rods of Authority, and this I fastened about five feet from the side by means of a couple of stout ash saplings. I found these improvements so admirable, that I was not afraid in light winds (having gained a knowledge of the tides and currents) of venturing anywhere either around Jethou or Herm.

Immense quantities of fish are found all round

Jethou, the principal being lobsters, crabs, crayfish, spider crabs, plaice, John Dorey, soles, ormers, pollock, bass, gurnard, skate, cod, long-nose, rock fish, turbot, brill, whiting, and conger.

Several of the fish I had never seen before, as they are rarely if ever caught off the Norfolk coast; thus John Dorey, spiders, ormers, rock fish, and pollock were all new to me, and gave me great enjoyment in their capture, beside which I was greatly taken with the flavour of both the Dorey and pollock, scores of which I caught in the Percée.

The ormer, rarely seen in England, is, I believe, sometimes called the Sea Ear. It is somewhat the shape and size of a half cocoa nut (divided lengthwise). The outside of the shell is of a rough texture, and of a dull red colour, while the inside is beautifully coloured with an iridescent mother o' pearl coating. (Why do we never hear anything of the father o' pearl?) The ormer adheres to the rocks like the limpet tribe, but is seldom seen above *low* water-mark, like the limpet, who loves to be exposed to the sun and air twice a day.

The flesh of the ormer, when grilled, is something like a veal cutlet cooked in a fishy frying-pan, and I cannot say I was greatly enraptured with the uncommon univalve.

My first meeting with the ormer was by accident. I was having an *al fresco* lunch of bread and raw limpets which I was detaching from the rocks, eating them with a seasoning of vinegar and pepper which I had brought with me when, being close down to the water among some outlying rocks (as it was a very low neap tide), I saw something just under the surface of a pool, of a dull red colour, which I perceived to be a shell-fish of some kind. Stooping down, with a rapid blow of my knife I detached it, and ere it sank into the unknown depths of the pool, plunged in my left hand and secured it. It was an ormer—at least, so I supposed, and on this supposition took it home and compared it with a book on shells I had, and being satisfied with my researches, cooked and ate the mollusc, although in some doubt. Next day, feeling much as the first man who ever swallowed an oyster did—alive and hearty—I went at dead low tide and gathered some more and ate also, but finally came to the conclusion that one good sole was worth a sack of ormers. Still, there is no accounting for taste. Some of the islanders are very fond of ormers; but what is one man's meat is another's "*poisson.*"

Although at neap tide on many occasions I gathered many more, it was more for the beauty of the shells than the flavour of the fish inside them.

For one with artistic tastes and love of colour like myself, the interior of an ormer shell is a veritable fairy grotto. One discovery I made regarding them and that is, that they form a dainty dish for the huge conger eels which abound among the rocks, and about this bait I must presently tell a little more.

The granite rocks below high water-mark are simply spotted all over with myriads of limpets, some of them of enormous size. Many of the shells in my collection are over three inches across, and the fish when cooked make two ample mouthfuls. My manner of dressing them was to place them in a tub of sea water for a night, and then to lay them on a gridiron, point downward, over a bright fire, and grill them. When cooked they would drop out of their shells when turned upside down over a plate containing vinegar and pepper, and I considered them very nice. A friend of mine who has tasted them in Cornwall says they would make any well-bred dog sick. Thus, I say again, tastes vary!

I must allow, however, that the leathery limpet is as far behind the delicious sole or turbot in flavour, as a turnip is inferior to an apple; but still a change is desirable, and for the matter of change I think I had a turn at everything eatable on the island or in the sea surrounding it, and still live to tell the tale.

Well, now, let me tell an adventure that befell me while conger fishing off the Crevichon one calm evening just after dark. First let me point out a device I had to adopt because my canoe had not sufficient space to hold or carry all the fish I sometimes caught. I had to have recourse to a floating fish carrier, and this I contrived out of an old dry goods box, which I bored full of holes, so as to allow a current of water to flow through and keep my fish alive. To give floating power to this *fish-pound*, I fastened large bungs all round the outside, and to each of the four corners I attached an inflated bladder, so that I could easily store in it from thirty to forty pounds of fish, as it must be observed, that whilst *in* the water the fish will swim, and thus add but little weight to their floating prison. This box I attached to the outrigger by a stout lanyard, and fended it off with the paddle, if the eddy brought it in too close proximity to my craft.

Well, to my fish story. I had been anchored for about two hours near Rocher Rouge fishing for conger, of which I had caught three small ones, beside several rock fish and whiting, when I thought I would try another kind of bait, so I armed my hook with a small ormer, which being of a gristly texture, held on the barb well. Over the side went the gear, attached to a strong line of thick water-cord, and although it was down a considerable time no warning tug gave hope of sport to follow, so I busied myself with the other two lines I had down, with a fair amount of success. At length getting tired of taking nothing on my big line, I thought I would coil it up and examine the bait, but when I had got the line straight up and down it refused to leave the bottom, tug as I would. I pulled till my canoe danced and bobbed about in an alarming manner, in fact, till the coaming was in danger of going under the gently heaving sea, but to no purpose; it would not budge, so tripping anchor I paid out line and paddled fifty yards, thinking that if my hook had fouled a rock I might by a side pull clear it. I hauled in gently, and to my surprise found the line come in with a curious vibrating motion, in little jerks, till it got straight up and down again, and then I had a hard pull to get it from the bottom; but still I did get it up little by little, and was now positive that it was a fish of some kind, and of great weight. Foot after foot of line came in very spasmodically, and with great reluctance, till at last a great, ugly, slimy head, with yellow-green eyes, came above the surface, and so large did it appear, that it quite took me aback. In my surprise I let go several

coils of the line before I knew what I was about. The head was enormous and *ex pede Hercules*. I knew the body must be of gigantic proportions too. That I had hooked one of Neptune's fiends seemed certain, and I was some time before I hauled up again to see really what I had captured. In came the line again, foot by foot, with great difficulty, till at length up came the terrible head again. But this time I was prepared, and setting my teeth, held on. It was a huge conger, such as I had never seen before, and which came very near being the last I might gaze upon, for suddenly it brought its tail up over the outrigger, and before I could counterbalance my craft, seemed to swamp the canoe by its dead weight and the power of its fins. I was in the water in a second, but never loosened my hold of the line. Letting go the loose coils I struck out for Rocher Rouge, only some fifty yards away, and, landing at the foot of the great granite throne, commenced to haul in my line. To my joy the canoe, which still floated with its coamings out of water, although the well was full, followed my line. I afterwards ascertained that in falling overboard I had dropped between the canoe and outrigger, and had thus drawn the line through the intervening space after me. To this fact I owed the recovery of my craft, which would otherwise have floated away, as I should have been afraid to follow it, although an excellent swimmer, as the currents are here so strong that I should probably never have got back again.

The canoe came slowly in till it was within reach, when I seized it, and with a mighty effort dragged it ashore undamaged. The lines I also drew in and coiled tidily away, leaving the long one till the last, which, to my great surprise, when I hauled in, still had the monstrous eel in tow. I quite thought he had freed himself when he swamped me, but such was evidently not the case. Having a firm footing I hauled in my line with more confidence, and at length got my lord close to the rocks, and in the clear water could see his huge length and thickness. He was a terrible fellow, and if he had got my legs in his embrace might have easily drowned me; but I did not give him a chance to use either his tail or teeth, but getting his head close to the rocks I took a turn of the line round a projecting crag, and proceeded to slaughter the monster with my only weapon, the paddle. He took a lot of assassinating, but gave up the ghost at last, after I had nearly pounded his head to a jelly.

Old "Begum," I must mention, witnessed my sudden departure from my canoe, and the dear old fellow arrived at Rocher Rouge at the same moment that I landed, so that we faced each other dripping wet in a most comical manner. I sent "Begum" to fetch "Eddy," and in the meantime emptied the canoe and put all straight, so that when the two animals appeared on the cliff, standing out in bold relief against the clear sky, I was in my canoe and on the way to the Cotills. They followed me till I landed, and came and stood by me like two old comrades. I had dragged the conger after me through the sea with a cord through his gills, and this cord I attached to "Eddy," who dragged him home in triumph, while

I sat on his back, *à la conqueror*, as I rode into my domain, tired and wet, and as hungry as the proverbial hunter.

A cheerful blaze of wood soon caused the kettle to boil, and over my tea-supper I congratulated myself over my lucky adventure, for to lose neither fish, canoe, nor self, was indeed a large slice of luck.

Next day I improvised a pair of scales with the help of a half hundredweight and a seven-pound weight which I possessed, and found to my surprise that the monster weighed one hundred and three pounds. This was not only the largest eel I ever caught, but the largest I ever saw. In Guernsey market the heaviest conger I saw was one of sixty-seven pounds—a baby in comparison to mine!

The weights I used in weighing the monster were stones adjusted to the proper iron weights, which I used as standards, and then by selecting various sized stones obtained after great toil a whole set, from one pound up to ten pounds, and thus could weigh anything.

I had many other fishing adventures, but I think the above was about the most exciting. I had many good takes of whiting and pollock, but was not so fortunate among the soles, and plaice, and such-like ground game, as my net was a very ramshackle affair of my own construction.

I had also some remarkable miscellaneous captures at different times. Once in the winter I had laid a long line for codling, and brought up, firmly hooked, a very nice red tablecloth, beautifully worked round the edge by some skilled hand in an Oriental pattern. I used it on gala days as a flag, and I dare say passers by in the various vessels wondered to what nationality it belonged, as the centre was ornamented with a golden elephant with very curly tusks worked in white beads. Another day I fished up a copper oil can, such as engineers use to oil machinery with; and yet another time a bag of gravel which had apparently once formed part of a yacht's ballast.

When I found time heavy on my hands I would often take my canoe about fifty yards south of La Fauconnaire, and with two or three lines fish for rock fish, and never, on a single occasion, returned empty-handed. The worst part of this performance was digging the bait of lugworms on the little beach of Creviçhon. It was terribly hard work lifting the rocks and boulders aside to find a place to dig, and then it was harder work in digging the nasty worms from the granite grit in which they resided, dwelt, or had their horrid being. Probably these hairy, oozy creatures have their joys and pleasures, and their woes, just as every other of God's creatures, but of what their happiness consists who can tell? Anyway they are good for bait, and so have use if not beauty to commend them.

Crabs and lobsters I could trap at any time by putting down "pots" anywhere round the island; but after a few weeks I got quite tired of them for the table, but would occasionally put down a couple of "pots" to see what of a curious nature I could catch. The crayfish, spider-crabs, and hermit crabs, gave me infinite amusement, as they are so different in their manners and customs to the ordinary crabs, and are very bellicose, going for each other tooth and nail, or rather legs and claws, in a most terrible manner. The way these little crustaceans maimed each other put me in mind of the scene in Scott's "Fair Maid of Perth," where the rival clans hew each others' limbs off with double-handed swords, so that a truce has to be called for the purpose of clearing the battle-ground of human *debris*. The crabs have the advantage over the human species, insomuch that they can reproduce a lost limb.

Finding I could catch a large quantity of fish of all kinds, especially rock fish, which, being new to me, I greatly admired, I set about constructing a fish pond near the house.

These rock fish are a curiosity in the way of fish. They run from about six inches to two feet in length; weigh from a few ounces to a dozen pounds, and no two that I have ever caught are alike, either in colour or disposition of spots. They are spotty and speckly all over. Some have copper-coloured spots, some yellow, some brown, some green, some red, and some an assortment of colours, so that one never knows what colour is coming up next. Persons who are fond, when playing cards, of betting upon the colour of the trump to be turned up—black or red—would find the pastime of "backing their colour" infinitely varied, if they tried to guess the colour of the fish which would next appear.

My first fish pond, ten feet by five feet, was a failure, as it was leaky; but not to be beaten I commenced another and much larger one, sixteen feet by ten feet. I selected a site close above high water-mark, and commenced digging, and in fact worked a whole day at it, intending to line it with a mixture of sand and lime, of which I had several tubs for making mortar for repairing the brickwork of my homestead ; but that very evening I discovered a natural fish pond, or rather a pool, that could be turned into one by a little outlay of labour.

A cleft between two large rocks, separating them by about six feet, allowed the sea at high tide to flow into a pool at the foot of an amphitheatre of rocks, which gave a basin of water, at high tide, about twenty feet across. Here was a grand, natural fish pool, and I soon turned it into a comfortable home for my finny captures.

First at low tide I cleared the bottom of this pool, and made it deeper. Then, having previously made a huge batch of mortar, I set to work and built a wall of rock across the cleft, until I had raised it six feet high, taking great care to make it perfectly watertight. This I strengthened by laboriously placing blocks of stone on each side, so as to prevent the sea from toppling my mortar-built wall over. As a pond it was a perfect success, except in one particular, and that was that the water in time would evaporate, or become stale ; so I put my wits together and constructed a curious kind of mill pump, which worked with four wooden buckets upon an endless rope. It was jerky, but effective ; that is it was effective at high water, when the tide came up to my sea-wall. At this time the mill, being placed right for the wind, would commence to work, and the buckets to ascend and descend, and each shoot its gallon of water into the pond, till sometimes it was full to the brim, and even running over. Thus I could change the water at will. I was simply delighted, and fished from morning till night to stock my pool, and in a fortnight had specimens of all kinds, colours, and sizes. Eels, soles, whiting, dorey, pollock, long-nose, crabs, lobsters were all there, but to my mind the big blubber-lipped rock fish were the peacocks of my pool.

I was so fond of lingering by this pool to read, and smoke, and watch the fish, that I built myself a rock summer-house, and roofed it in with wood, upon which I placed a layer of mortar, and then thatched it with pine branches and braken. It was a picturesque little house, in a picturesque spot, and if I tell the truth, I believe I made a picturesque Crusoe.

My dress consisted, in summer, of white duck trousers, canvas shoes, coloured flannel shirt, a blue jean jacket, and broad-brimmed hat. Round my waist I always wore a long red sash; it was four yards long, consequently, would encircle my waist three times and still leave some of the two ends to hang down at my side. This sash I found very useful, for I used it as a wallet or hold-all. Nothing came amiss to it—tobacco, pipes, cartridges, biscuits, fruit, fishing tackle, all were tucked away in it at different or the same time, as they were so easy to get at, and left the hands free.

Now let us leave fish and fishing, and see in what other ways I enjoyed my solitary life.

CHAPTER VI.

"FLAP" THE GULL—SURGICAL OPERATION—THE GULL WHO REFUSED TO DIE—TAXIDERMY EXTRAORDINARY—FEATHERED FRIENDS—SNAKES.

EVERY part of the island swarmed with rabbits, in fact, it was a perfect warren, and must have contained thousands of them. I had therefore to devise some means of keeping them down, or they would so have multiplied as to eat up everything that to a rodent was toothsome, and that is *nearly* everything green, even to the furze bushes. I had only four tooth-traps with me, and these were not nearly adequate for the number I wanted to kill, so I had recourse to wire gins. These I soon became an adept in setting, and discovered that by placing the thin wire noose close to the ground I could catch the wee rabbits, while by keeping the lower part of the noose about four inches above the turf I could secure the large ones. By practice and observation I soon learned not only the best "runs," but could tell just where they would place their feet, as they bounded up or down the steep acclivities.

At times I had seventy or eighty gins set, and

caught perhaps a hundred a week in the season, which I regret to say were nearly all thrown into the sea. This destruction of good food I was very sorry to cause, as it would have fed a dozen poor families; but it was a case of kill the rabbits, or starve my own animals. I chose the latter alternative, and thus had plump animals and plump rabbits too. Those I retained formed food for myself, dog, pigs, and a gull I kept.

The gull I must say a little about, as he became a constant companion to me when I was within the wall which surrounded the homestead. "Flap," for so I christened him, was a large grey and white gull which I secured soon after coming to the island, by breaking his wing at a long shot. He tried, poor fellow, to scramble down to the sea, and swim away, but "Begum" was too quick for him, and pounced upon him before he could get over the rocks. I examined the bird and found the wing bone to be broken, but otherwise the bird was not at all hurt. It then came into my mind to perform a surgical operation, and this I quickly carried out. I trimmed away all the feathers from about the wound, and then with one draw of my sharp knife cut through the flesh between the smashed bone, and quickly amputated the wing.

"Flap" was so fierce, and had such a formidable bill, that I had to fasten him to a post to do all this, or he might have given me a deep wound. I then bathed the stump of the wing with warm water, and bound it up in a lump of lard, and the operation was complete.

I placed him in the stable and fed him with bits of fish, rabbit, and vegetable for about a week, by which time he was fairly tame; so then I took him out and fastened a leather strap round his leg, and tethered him on the grass plot in front of my house, as one would a cow, feeding him several times daily on animal food or fish. After a week of this he was so tame that he would try to get away from his peg to meet me in the morning. Seeing this, I decided to release him from his stake. I did so, and the poor bird followed me about like a dog; in fact, I believe "Begum" was jealous of him, for when I petted the gull he would come and thrust his great black nose into my hand, and look up to my eyes, as much as to say,

"Don't forget me, master!"

At the end of about three weeks I ventured to take the bandage off "Flap's" wing-stump, when I found, to my surprise, that it was so nearly healed as not to require further treatment from me, Harry Nilford, M.D.

"Flap's" domain was the homestead, about which he would hop and flap with his one wing in a most comical manner. If I threw down half a rabbit and called him, he would dash across the lawn at a gait that would defy description, while his voracity was wonderful to behold. He would take down half a rabbit in two or three fierce gulps, skin, bones, and flesh; and I have known him, when very hungry, to eat a whole one at a meal, which would only take a couple of minutes for him to discuss. It was simply a matter of Hey Presto! and his meal was consumed.

If a man could eat in the same proportion, half a sheep would make a meal, while a goose or turkey would only be a snack. Thank goodness, our appetites are less keen, or a fat bullock would only serve a large family for dinner, with the odds and ends left for supper.

"Begum" and "Flap" were fast friends, and the dog would allow the bird to take many liberties with him, such as taking quietly some pretty sharp pecks if he attempted to eat a bit of "Flap's" food; but on the other hand, "Flap" would take "Begum's" food from under his very nose without a protest of any kind from the dog, except a look out of the corner of his eye, as if he thought "What impudence!"

I found sea fowl of all kinds to be very tenacious of life, especially the common large gull. One case of this occurs to me as I write. I fired at a gull and brought it down on the rocks; but it was only winged, and picking it up, I wrung its neck, and flung it down, thinking it was dead, but in a couple of minutes it gave such signs of returning animation that I put the butt of my gun on its neck, which was upon the hard pathway, and pressed with all my might. But the thing would *not* die, so I got cross with both it and myself, with the bird for not dying and myself for causing it so much unnecessary pain. Thinking to kill the bird instantaneously, I took out my penknife, and ran it (or supposed I was in the right spot) quite through the brain, so that the blade projected half an inch on the other side. Just then some more gulls came within shot, and I threw the bird on the ground, and made an onslaught on the others. I dropped one, and scrambled down the cliffs for it, and at length having secured it, climbed laboriously up the steep rocks again. Judge of my surprise when, puffing and blowing from my exertions, just as my head rose above the ledge of the pathway where I had left the transfixed bird, I saw it rise to its feet, give a loud Quah! and before I could prevent it, away it went, half flying and flopping, half running and scrambling, with my knife still in its skull, and was quickly out of sight.

The different kinds of gulls visiting Jethou are very numerous, and some of them very pretty. One of the finest being the swift sea swallow, with its lovely grey feathers, forked tail, and long graceful wings. Another is the sea-pie, a very shapely black and white gull, which makes a noise quite peculiar to itself when hunting among the rocky inlets for its food, thus betraying its presence.

Whenever I killed a bird of which I did not know the name, I would fasten it up to some sticks in as life-like manner as possible, and make a water colour drawing of it, taking great care to shew every detail, so that in time I had over thirty drawings, each of which took me half a day to execute. These are now in the writer's possession, and form a pretty memento of his Crusoe days.

I took to making these drawings, because my attempts at taxidermy were grotesquely ludicrous; to put it plainly, they were unmitigated failures. These remarks apply to my very early attempts, for I would not have the readers think me incapable after long practice of turning out a shapely bird or a fish fair to behold. I must own that my early struggles at skinning and stuffing were certainly funny, as except from the colour of the feathers one could not tell a tern from a Kentish crow after I had mangled it about for a few hours. They were wonders of natural history these specimens of mine, not altogether from my unskilfulness in handling them, but from the fact that I lacked materials to work with. During the long nights of autumn, I, to a certain extent, perfected myself in setting up specimens, but found they would not keep, as I had no arsenic to work with, using in its place a disinfectant which was not a preservative, consequently my specimens began to get mouldy and to smell high, and this prevailing mustiness brought them to an untimely end, or at least the greater portion of them. Thinking a day in the sunshine and fresh air might improve them, I took them all out of the house, and carried them a few at a time down to the small lawn, as it was nice and open, placing them promiscuously down on the green sward; and a funny lot they looked. Fish of all kinds, condition, and colors, and birds in all positions, natural and unnatural; the Chamber of Horrors at Madame Tussaud's Waxworks was a pleasant sight in comparison to my collection, at least that was the impression I gleaned from "Begum" and "Flap," both of whom seemed perfectly mad at seeing such an array of scarecrows on their favourite playground.

It was a lovely mild day, and I spent best part of it at La Fauconnaire, rabbit and gull shooting, bringing home for my day's sport as many as I could fairly carry. Leaving them in the storehouse I fed

"Eddy," and proceeded to perform the same office for the goat and pigs, but they were nowhere to be seen. After a fair amount of searching I gave them up for the time, and proceeded to take in my stuffed wonders, but alas, the pigs and goat had been before me, for in the morning I had not properly latched the lawn gate, and they had got in and created awful havoc. Many of my specimens the pigs had actually eaten, others they had disjointed and mangled in such a manner as to be perfectly useless, while what they had not fallen foul of my Quixotic goat had, by spiking them with her single horn, till she had had the satisfaction of knocking the stuffing out of them. What was left of my most magnificent collection now looked as if a charge of dynamite had played havoc with it. Thus my friends and the world in general were prevented from gazing upon one of the most curious collections of birds, beasts, and fishes that have ever been stuffed (with whatever was handiest) since the art of taxidermy was introduced.

The stormy petrel during rough weather used to be a frequent visitor to the Perchée Channel, skimming just above the dark waves so close to the surface, as to appear to walk up a wave, rise above its crest, and then walk down into the valley of water on the opposite side. I shot several specimens, two of which I stuffed, but they were both eaten by those horrid pigs.

Oyster-pickers were quite plentiful, and I quickly discovered that they might also aptly be termed limpet-pickers, for they seemed to take these shell fish as their staple food. The *modus operandi* of feeding is to pounce down upon a rock which the receding tide has left bare, and with a single sharp blow with its beak, detach a limpet, and turning it mouth upward, pick out the fish at its leisure. If it failed to detach the limpet at once it would go on to another, knowing that when once disturbed the limpet requires great force to detach it. Oysters lie in deep waters where they are inacessible to these birds, so whence is their name derived?

Then there were various kinds of divers, the principal of which class was the cormorant, greatly resembling a half-starved black swan, that is, it had a longer and thinner and less graceful body; but in many points it was superior to the swan, especially in its flying and diving powers, and in its quickness of action. Its head appears never to be still, but constantly bobbing and turning from side to side, as if saying, "Did you ever catch a cormorant asleep?" Knowing that the Chinese train these birds to catch fish, I endeavoured to induce one to come to me, and serve his apprenticeship as a fisherman, but to no purpose. It was just as well I could not catch one, for I find they must be trained from their young days to the art, as they are intractable in their grown-up wildness, and I was thus spared a great deal of unnecessary trouble and irritability of temper.

Although I had a store of simple medicines with me, I scarcely ever required to open the case. Once and once only, I felt poorly for a whole week, but that I fancy was attributable to fruit and the heat. Although not well, I thoroughly enjoyed a whole lazy week, most of which I spent by the side of my fish pool, studying the habits of my finny comrades in captivity. Some of the rock fish became so tame that they would rise to the surface when I dropped crumbs of biscuits on the water, and I verily believe if I had had the patience, I might have taught them to feed from my fingers. Sometimes for a treat I would bring "Flap" and place him near the water, and he seemed to enjoy looking at the denizens; but they were all too big for him to gobble, or he would have made an Aldermanic dinner of some of them.

I occasionally saw a snake, but always of the harmless, blindworm variety. Of this species I caught two and admired them, but I did not make pets of them as I did of nearly everything else I could lay hands on.

One big fellow nearly two feet long I threw into the sea, thinking to rid the island of at least one snake; but to my surprise he swam ashore on the surface of the water as quickly as he could have progressed on dry land. He was a veritable sea-serpent, although a small specimen.

There were also two kinds of lizards of which I do not know the name, but they were only small fellows, and may be what are called "efts." They would sun themselves on the warm rocks, and on being disturbed dart into some cranny till danger was past. They ran up and down rocks which were nearly perpendicular, and were very amusing in their rapid movements.

I often thought as I lay in my hammock how I should have liked a squirrel or two to be climbing about the branches above me; but one is never contented with what is allotted them. Probably had I possessed a squirrel or two, I should have longed for a few monkeys, and having them, should have wished for something else.

Altogether I was perfectly contented with my lot, especially after the melancholy of the first week had worn off, except just now and again a particularly dismal feeling would assert itself, which I could not shake off; but I simply attributed this to dull weather or over exertion. It was nothing worth mentioning.

My spirits are like a barometer; when the sun shines and the weather is warm I am up; when it is wet and dull I am down, and I think this is the case with many persons; in fact, I believe weather has a greater influence on our lives than we are aware of. Statistics go to prove this; for instance, more marriages take place during the five months, June to September, than in the other seven colder months. From gaiety to despair,—more suicides take place at the fall of the year than at any other period. Rodent slaughter commenced this chapter and suicide ends it; this puts me in mind of the Marriage Service, which commences "Dearly" and ends with "amazement."

CHAPTER VII.

I BUILD A CURIOUS "BOX" BOAT—AN UNPLEASANT NIGHT AT SEA—MY SUNDAY SERVICE—THE POEM, "ALEXANDER SELKIRK"—ITS APPLICABILITY TO MY LOT.

DURING the summer my roving propensities began to assert themselves, and I longed to go farther *afield* over the sea. I bethought me how I might contrive myself a boat in which to venture into the offing with, as my canoe was too frail to go far from shore.

I looked around to see what I could utilize, and found I had a few inch boards and plenty of rivets, nails, and screws; but after overhauling my stock I came to the conclusion that my materials would not warrant my commencing a craft of any size, so for several days I gave up the project, till one day visiting the boathouse I cast my eyes on the large tin-lined packing cases in which my goods had been packed. Why not utilize these? There were four of them. Three were of the same dimensions, namely, four feet long, three feet wide, and two and a half feet deep; while the fourth was three feet and a half long, two feet wide, and two and a half feet deep.

F

That night I went to bed early, so as to have a good "think" as to how I could make a boat of these boxes, with the help of my deal boards and tools.

I soon hit on a plan, and could scarcely get a wink of sleep for thinking and maturing my plans; in fact, at two a.m. I got up, dressed, and went and re-measured the cases and re-inspected them, to see if they were really eligible for my purpose. They were, and I retired to bed again perfectly overjoyed, so that I only dozed and woke continually till five a.m., when I finally arose and commenced operations in the boathouse.

"Begum" knew there was something in the wind, for I had little to say to him, so full was I of my scheme.

I found my cases with their tin linings were quite water-tight, which was a necessary condition for keeping my craft afloat, and having prepared my tools and got my timber ready for a start, went homeward to breakfast, shooting a very fine pigeon on the way, which had probably strayed over from Guernsey. Here was a dinner provided for me which only required cooking. Indeed, it frequently happened that at breakfast time my dinner would be flying about round the island.

To help me in the description of the building of my craft I here give sketches of her construction. First I took my cases 2, 3, and 4, and firmly screwed them together, and afterwards added number 5, which was not so wide by six inches, but still served admirably for a stern. Then came my first difficulty. How should I form the bows? This I got over by making another case, No. 1, of a triangular form with a bulkhead running across, to which I nailed my side timbers, so as to give them an outward curve. These streaks I put on clinker-wise—that is, overlapping, and thoroughly caulked them with oakum soaked in grease.

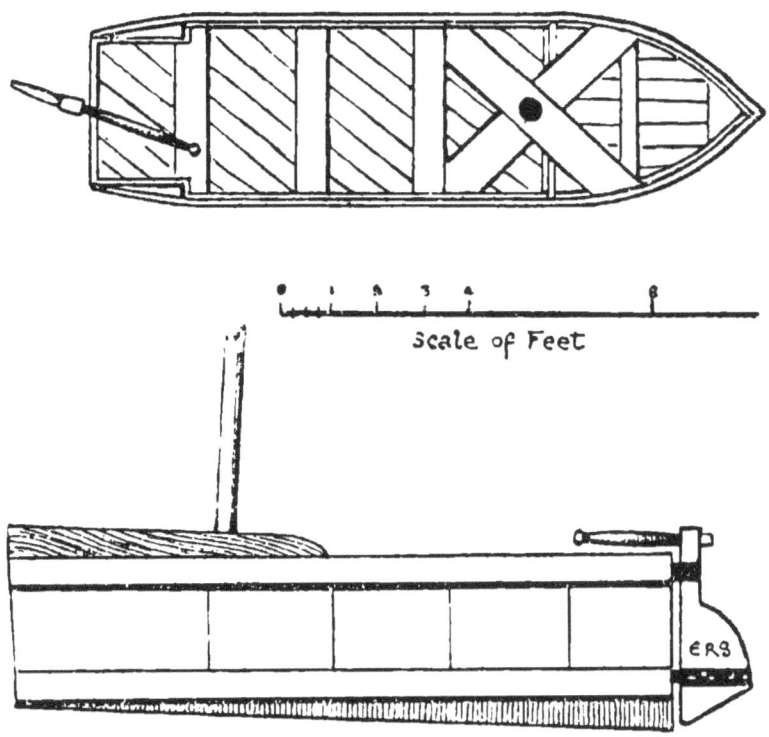

The YELLOW-BOY

Next, to strengthen the hull and hold everything firmly in position, I nailed a top streak along from stem to stern, so as to form a gunwale, and another at the lower edges of the cases, tarring everything as I proceeded, including myself; but as the weather was hot a pair of old pants cut off at the knee, and a ragged shirt, were my only encumbrance in the way of clothing. Now I proceeded to cut down the partitions between the various sections for a depth of six inches. I then carefully caulked the tiny crack between each of these bulkheads, and turning the surplus tin over, nailed it to the wood. Over these bulkheads I placed thwarts six inches wide, and then proceeded to make a keel. This I did by bolting two thicknesses of board together and cutting them down, so that it measured three inches deep at the stem and six at the stern. The fastening on of this keel gave me more trouble than anything else connected with the boat, for I had no bolts long enough to go through six inches of timber, and then through the bottom of the boat. There was only one way, and that was to make some bolts eight inches long, and this I did from some pieces of three-eight iron rod I found. Nine bolts took me a whole day to make—from six in the morning till six in the evening. My anvil was a granite rock, which I had to carry on my shoulders from the beach; but it served its purpose capitally.

My labours at the anvil were considerably lightened by the singing of all the appropriate songs I could think of, especially the "Village Blacksmith," which I think I must have worn out while making my bolts and other fastenings.

I made heads to my bolts, and thrusting them through the keel, fastened them off on the inside with iron collars or burrs. To make the keel more secure I ran a strap of iron up the stern, from the heel of the keel, and screwed it in place.

For the mast I made a step by crossing two pieces of board, and where they crossed cut a hole through sufficiently large to take my mast, which was a short one, being only about ten feet long. These cross pieces not only held the mast, but also greatly strengthened the bows, which felt the first and full force of the waves.

Then the rudder had to be made and attached, thole pins provided, and the whole concern tarred inside and out, tin and all.

Oars had to be made, and with these I had some little difficulty; but by steadily pegging away I at length turned out three very serviceable, if not elegant, ones. The third was in case of a breakage, for it would never do to go to sea without a spare oar, as in case of accident I might have drifted helplessly goodness knows where.*

The Bay of Avranches is a large place, and as the Channel Islands do not lie in the direct course of ocean-going vessels, it would be extremely awkward, even on a calm day, to be alone in a boat with but one oar.

I found a large roll of old sails in the loft of the boathouse, all much too large for my boat; but I selected a jib, and cut it down to form a lug-sail.

---

* It so happened that only a few years since, a young lady, taking a row after church one Sunday evening, lost an oar overboard and drifted out to sea. In the morning she was picked up (being then quite out of sight of land) by a vessel bound for Canada, and actually taken to Newfoundland, from whence in about a month she arrived home safely, much to the joy of her sorrowing friends, who had given her up as drowned.

This sail being discoloured, I gave it a coat of yellow ochre and boiled oil on each side, which gave it a very curious appearance. The upper strake of my boat I also painted yellow, and to finish off christened my craft the "Yellow Boy."

The launch was a Herculean task, as I had built her too high above high water-mark, and it took me nearly a day to get her down and afloat. Finding I could not move her with my own bodily strength, I had to carry an anchor out and attach a block-tackle and thus, with the help of my faithful old comrade, "Eddy," haul the boat gradually down below high water-mark, where I left her for the tide to rise and float her. She seemed large while I was at work upon her, but the huge bulk of Crevichon towering up in the background dwarfed her to a cockle shell.

While the tide was rising I busied myself in selecting large flat pieces of granite for ballast, and fastening them down to the floor with battens, which operation was scarcely finished when the tide came into the little cove, and in half an hour the "Yellow Boy" was afloat. "Hurrah!" I shouted, while "Begum" barked with joy. I could not refrain from taking the good fellow with me for the trial trip, for I must have someone to talk to, as I felt in such a joyful mood.

It was late in the afternoon when we started off, and I had not broken my fast since dinner, so letting the boat drift on the now sluggish tide, I opened my tin provision box, and with capital appetites my dog and I fell to.

The water found its way in in two or three places,

but these I quickly caulked, and soon had everything water-tight. Then the sail did not sit to my liking, so down it came, and having my palm and needles I soon altered it. Then I shifted the ballast somewhat, and got everything square and snug.

After about a couple of hours, as the tide was quite spent, I thought it was about time to turn towards home, but on looking back the islands had disappeared in the evening haze which was springing up, so turning the boat's head I guessed at the position of Jethou, and hauled up the sail. There was but a breath of wind, and before half an hour of our homeward voyage was accomplished it was (with the sea fog and the approach of night) quite dark. Still I kept on, not sure where I was going, as I could not see a light anywhere, till presently a steady rain set in, and then I knew we were in for a night of it. The weather was warmish, but I was so lightly clothed that I was quickly drenched to the skin. I looked eagerly for a ship's light, but not one could I see, or I would have borne down upon her and got the bearings of Jethou from her skipper. I did what best I could under the circumstances, resolving never again to be led away by any new fad, so as to be oblivious to everything else, as I had been in getting my new boat into trim. It was a dreadful time for me, as I knew Jethou to be surrounded by rocks on all sides, so that I had to keep a very sharp look out, for fear of running on them and getting stove in, which would probably have resulted in my death, if the rocks were submerged at high water.

About what I should judge to be the middle of the

night, as I sat shaking with cold with my hand on the tiller, I suddenly became aware of the presence of huge rocks right in front of me. I lowered the sail instantly and got out the oars, pulling gently to the lee side of these rocks, and with some difficulty landed and made fast my boat between two lofty pillars of granite, which rose sheer from the sea. I was dreadfully cold and could find no shelter from the rain, which had completely saturated my paltry clothing. I therefore had a dip in the sea, which appeared to me warmer than the cold rain and night air, and less likely to have bad after effects upon my constitution. Oh, poor Robinson Crusoe! here was a pretty kettle of fish at the very first trip. How gladly would I have changed places with my donkey, who was safely under shelter, listening to the rain beating down, and saying to himself, "No work for me to-morrow!"

The longest night must have an end, although I began to fear this particular one would not do so, till I was past caring whether the sun ever rose again or not. But by-and-bye the dawn began to break, and quickly spread itself over the sky, and with the light the fog dispersed slowly, and showed me a barrel upon the top of a pole perched on the highest rock of the group I was a prisoner upon, by which I knew I was on the Ferriers, which lie about a short mile southwest of Jethou. I climbed to the pole and took a survey, and could just make out Jethou's back above the haze which still rolled silently above the still waters.

Down I scrambled to my boat, eager to push off and reach home, but alas, my craft was high and dry four feet above the sea, on a ledge which just held her comfortably cradled, in derision to my anxiety. "Begum" lay calmly sleeping in the stern sheets. How I envied him his power of passing the dull hours away, oblivious to wet or cold.

Half an hour—an hour—two hours passed, and then the kindly sea had compassion on my lonely, forlorn condition, and rose and toyed with my boat, and finally lifted her and bore her safely back to my home.

Home! what a word after such a night! I almost fell ashore, so great was my anxiety, and so desperately hungry did I feel.

My surroundings had now changed from what they were three hours since; for now I was on my island home, with the birds singing and the sun shining brightly and warmly upon me, so that I threw off my wet clothes and worked in a state of nature to get my tackle ashore, while "Begum" fetched "Eddy" to help me to get my craft above tide mark.

Good old "Eddy." I felt he was indeed a friend as he came trotting down the rocky path with a regular royal salute of braying. He tugged, and I tugged, till when the boat was safely beached I felt as nearly exhausted as ever I have been in my life. I scarcely had strength to get up the path which usually I took at a run. However, I *did* get up, and took a good nip of brandy, following it with some solid refreshment, eating as I lit the copper fire and filled the copper with water. While I waited for the water to become hot, I became so drowsy that I could scarcely keep awake, and yawned till an observer might have seen the roots of my hair, such an open countenance did I present. The water (although I watched it) boiled at last, and this I poured into a big tub partly filled with cold water, and had a bath for ten minutes as hot as I could bear it, after which I hopped into bed and slept, and slept, and slept.

It was eight a.m. when I went to bed, and I did not wake for fourteen hours—that is till ten p.m.; and knowing that I had slept the entire day away without a thought for my poor live stock, I turned over, resolving to be up and feed the said live stock at dawn. But when I again woke the sun was high above the horizon, and up I jumped, or tried to, but found that I was very stiff and sore all over from my night adventure. As I walked about and worked, feeding my animals, I gradually felt better, especially after a hearty breakfast, of which I stood much in need, after twenty-four hours' fast.

After this adventure I was very careful not to go out again without protection from the weather in the shape of a good thick coat and sou'wester, beside which I always put a tin of biscuits and a two-pound tin of preserved meat in the lockers near the stern, in case of emergency, and more than once I had to break bulk when a trip unexpectedly kept me out longer than I anticipated.

I now had all I could desire in the way of comforts and engagements, and not an idle day did I spend, except Sundays, upon which day I never did a stroke of work nor fired a shot. Even my rabbit gins were neglected that day. All I did was to feed my animals, walk or doze in my hammock and meditate, and this to me was a great enjoyment. When the wind was westerly I could hear the Guernsey church bells ringing for service, and when they ceased I knew it was eleven o'clock, and regulated my watch accordingly; that being done I always spent the time between that hour and twelve in going through the church service for the day, and the regulation three hymns, with one or two added, and a chapter or two from the Bible in place of a sermon. Then I felt comfortable, and contented, and without fear.

One Sunday afternoon, swinging in my hammock in the grove reading a book of poetry, I came across those beautiful verses by Cowper, entitled, "Alexander Selkirk," and could not but think how true they were to my own lot in many points; in fact, few persons reading the poem *could* appreciate it as I did in my solitude, with nought but the sea and sky with their teeming creatures around me. The first half of the first verse fitted me capitally, and I could not get it out of my head all day; it tickled my fancy:

> "I am monarch of all I survey,
>   To my right there is none to dispute;
> From the centre all round to the sea,
>   I am lord of both fowl and of brute."

In the second verse occur the lines:

> "I am out of humanity's reach,
>   I must finish my journey alone;
> Never hear the sweet music of speech—
>   I start at the sound of my own."

Certainly it was very seldom I heard a human voice,

even in the distance, sometimes not for weeks together; but as to starting at the sound of my own, well, that is not at all correct. Probably if my friends could have heard the voice of either " Eddy " or myself, when in full song, *they* would have had a *start*, if not a severe shock to the system.

Again :

> " Society, friendship, and love,
>   Divinely bestowed upon men ;
> Oh, had I the wings of a dove,
>   How soon would I taste you again ! "

Dove's wings would not have borne my thirteen stone weight. Perchance the giant wings of the Albatross would have been more practicable, if less poetical, and with these appendages I might have been tempted to have a peep at my friends in England, despite the supremely ridiculous figure I should have cut in the air, and the chance I should have stood of being shot as a very *rara avis*. Fancy me lighting down on our old thatched-roof house, and frightening everyone out of their seven senses, including my darling Priscilla, who, if she were not too frightened, would certainly bring me down with a charge of No. 4 (chilled) shot.

The next verse is nearly true of my state in its entirety :

> " Religion ! what treasure untold
>   Resides in that heavenly word !
> More precious than silver and gold,
>   Or all that this earth can afford ;

> But the sound of the church-going bell
> These valleys and rocks never heard;
> Never sighed at the sound of a knell,
> Or smiled when a Sabbath appeared."

It is scarcely true to say that the rocks *never* hear the sound of the church-going bell, for with a westerly breeze the bells can be heard quite plainly, and I have even heard a dog bark at that distance, which shows how distinctly, and to what a great distance sound will travel over water.

If rocks have ears they must occasionally have been ravished by my rendering of Sankey and Moody's hymns. If they have a memory they must have learnt several of them by heart; in fact, have been so familiar with them as to desire a change for something secular. They never applauded me, but when the Heavens spoke with thunder they clapped their granite hands till they cracked again.

The last verse hits me again—quite a bull's eye:

> "But the sea fowl is gone to her nest,
> The beast is laid down in his lair;
> Even here is a season of rest,
> And I to my cabin repair.
> There's mercy in every place,
> And mercy, encouraging thought!
> Gives even afiliction a grace,
> And reconciles man to his lot."

Yes, I nightly had to repair to my cabin, and in the wet season had my cabin to repair; but I made it so cosy, that like the last line, "it reconciled me to my lot."

Oh, Crusoe! how I would have loved to have shared Juan Fernandez with thee! What a Friday I would have been, and what enjoyment I should have discovered in everything—except black man killing! But even that I should have taken my part in it if it came to the question "kill or be killed."

CHAPTER VIII.

A TRIP TO ST. SAMPSON'S HARBOUR—A HORRID PORCINE MURDER—A VOYAGE ROUND SARK—NEARLY CAPSIZED—TRIP ROUND GUERNSEY—THE PEPPER-BOX—CURIOSITY OF TOURISTS.

FROM time to time I made many improvements in the "Yellow Boy," and learnt her capabilities, so that in time I took quite long cruises as far as Guernsey, and even to Sark.

It will be remembered that two of the conditions my father imposed upon me, were that I should not land on any other island nor speak to anyone under any pretence whatever, and these rules I rigorously carried out. Many a time passing boatmen hailed me, but a wave of the hand and my finger pointed to my output tongue was the only answer they received, consequently I was called the "Dumb Man of Jethou," or the "Yellow Boy," and as such and by no other name many of the fishermen knew me. Those who did not know my history pitied me as a kind of voiceless castaway or semi-sane being.

My long trips were sometimes undertaken on calm moonlight nights: one, I remember, was to St.

Sampson's Harbour, Guernsey. I started about three a.m., and reached the harbour before four o'clock, so that I had a good look around the little haven, and at the shipping before anyone was astir. I moored to the cable of a big brigantine which was lying alongside the wharf ready for her cargo of granite for London. Curb stones, blocks for paving, and broken metal for macadam roads are all shipped here to the amount of several thousand tons weekly, so that the granite quarrying and dressing give occupation to about 2,000 men, women, and children. Granite working and fruit growing are the two great industries of the island, which seems to me to be composed principally of two extremely different materials—granite and glass; at any rate it is not the place for stone throwing.

As I swung on the cable of the big ship, I made myself a cup of coffee; for I always carried a small lamp stove with me, so that I could cook the fish I caught fresh from the sea, or make myself a cup of tea or coffee to wash my meal down with.

I have since found, that within the memory of persons still alive, Guernsey was nearly cut off from Vale Parish by an arm of the sea, which flowed over the salt marshes at high tide, so that all communication was cut off between the two parts of the island except by one little bridge and the ferry boat. The bridge was about 380 yards west of St. Sampson's Church; but at the present day pleasant meadows, houses, and roads take the place of the broad stream of salt water and marshes, which formerly made Guernsey and Vale separate islands twice a day, at the time of high tide.

Just before five o'clock when heads began to peep over bulwarks, and men to appear on the quay, passing to their work, I thought it time to be off, as my strange craft would be sure to attract attention, which I did not court, so I packed up and made snug for sailing. I was only just in time, for a bearded face looked over the bulwarks of the brigantine, and hailed me with a "Good morning, mate!" but I only pointed to my mouth and ears as I unmoored. When I looked up again as I pushed off there were half a dozen merry faces peering over the side at me, and I could see they were surprised at the "Yellow Boy" and her dumb skipper. As I sculled out of the harbour I could hear their remarks and laughter, despite my deaf-mutism, and would gladly have had a chat with them if it had not been for my "rules," for these were the first human voices I had heard close by me for nearly four months.

Away I scudded, taking my way across the Little Russel, past the stone fort, with its one pop-gun on top, which is supposed to dominate the channel, standing as it does on a rocky islet midway between Guernsey and Herm. If a modern warship meant business, the bellicose gunners of this little inkpot-looking fort would have what the French call a *mauvais quart d'heure*. Arrived home about seven I had all the day before me. One of our poets says,

> "The only way to lengthen our days,
> Is to take a piece off of the night, my boys!"

This I used frequently to do, but always took care to take *my* piece off the night, so as to *prefix* the day

G

instead of making it a kind of baccanalian *appendix*. I have sometimes had my day twenty hours long, from two in the morning till ten at night; but with this I used afterwards to take an antidote in the shape of ten or eleven hours' sleep. On such occasions I always gave my animals a double allowance of food, and if they were improvident enough to consume it, as if it were carnival time, or a period of some great feast, that was their look out, and after their feast came a fast, which at worst only gave them an increased appetite, and did them no real harm.

Speaking of appetite and eating, I must describe my first pig-killing. I felt that I required pork, and the more I thought of it the more I was convinced that I *must* have it, although a murder had to be committed before I could have it either roast, boiled, or fried. Very well, what easier! There were the two pigs, each about one hundred and forty pounds weight; all I had to do was to kill one. Of course I would set about it at once; but upon reflection I became aware that some courage was required, and that I was totally ignorant of the work before me. However, I sharpened a long knife and went and had a look at the pigs, and the more I looked the less I liked my task; so much so, that after half an hour I decided that I would have tinned mutton for dinner—the pork would be too fresh, and perhaps it might be a dull day to-morrow, and I should want something to do! So the pig received a respite. Next morning when I awoke and considered how and when I should kill the pig, I made the resolve that come what might "that day the pig should die."

After breakfast I again sharpened the knife, as if it had become blunt again in the night, and got up a razor edge on the weapon, and once more proceeded to the stye. I selected my victim, and got one of my legs over the wall of the enclosure; but then my heart failed me, it seemed as if I was about to slay an old friend; indeed, they *were* old friends, those two piggies, and I had had many a chat with them, in fact, could almost understand their language of grunts.

How was I going to secure my victim before giving the *coup de grace?* Should he not be offered up on a stool? if so, I had not one to use; but an idea struck me, and that idea I adopted. Over the stye, about ten feet from the ground, the limb of a walnut tree stretched across, and my idea was to drop a line over the bough and make it fast round the porker's snout, haul him up on his hind legs, and bury my knife up to the hilt in his throat about where I thought his heart was situated. Away I went and procured my cord, threw the end over the limb, made a noose, and got it in the pig's mouth and over his nose; then I hauled away amid the most blood-curdling shrieks imaginable. I got him on his hind legs, and then for the first time, as I took the knife from my belt, I knew the full meaning of the word "coward." But the deed had to be done, it would never do to let the animal die of old age while I wanted meat; so, setting my teeth, plunge went the knife, and at the same time in my eagerness to step back, down I fell backward over the other pig, who turned and bit me in the thigh, and then as he rushed away went full butt into his comrade, which broke the rope, and down came the bleeding animal on top of me. I was in an awful state of filth, and as I rose they both came at me again; in fact I might have been seriously hurt had I not used my knife freely on the already-wounded pig. Luckily the other ran away, or it might have been serious for me. In falling a second time I went down with my leg under me, and could not rise; but I drove the knife into the animal's breast with all my might, and then, seizing him round the body with my arms, forced the hilt further in with my chest, but instead of killing the beast, to my horror the point came out of his back as he freed himself and walked away. I rose and got out of the stye as nimbly as I possibly could, and sat down to try and find my face through the accumulation of blood and filth, which having done, I peeped over the stye wall, and found the pig still alive; so, to end the poor thing's misery and my own, I took up my gun and shot him dead. What a relief it was to see him lie stone still in an instant. I vowed never to attempt a porcine murder again, and while I was on the island the other pig had a good time of it, for as governor of Jethou I abolished capital punishment, and if a pig's years were as many as Methuselah's, he might enjoy them all before I should again attempt to put a period to them.

From assassination to boat sailing is a long stride but at least a change.

I performed two long voyages in my little craft; at least they seemed long ones to me at the time, considering the dangers of navigation in these rocky, swift seas.

A PORCINE MURDER.

One trip was to Sark, which lies about six miles south-east of Jethou. I selected a beautiful day in August for this trip, and started at daylight, about four a.m., well provisioned, and with "Begum" to accompany me, for somehow I always felt safer with him beside me. A light south-west wind was blowing, so we reached Sark by six a.m., and mooring the boat at the foot of the Coupée, in a bay called Grand Gréve, I prepared coffee, and had a very leisurely breakfast, wondering at man's capacity for stowage; but that is due to the salt breeze which never yet put a man's liver wrong.

After enjoying the rocking in the bright warm sunshine, and watching the tiny people crossing the Coupée (like the little men crossing a bridge on a willow-patterned plate), three hundred feet overhead, off I started again. I kept about two hundred yards from the precipitous sides of the island, steering so close to the rock Moie de la Bretagne, which rises ninety feet above the sea, that I touched it as we (my boat, dog, and I) glided by.

Next, into the romantic little bay of Port Gorey (just a lovers' paradise), where I let "Begum" have a run ashore while I sketched. Here are situate the mines which were abandoned many years ago as a dismal failure, leaving as a legacy to those fond of sketching some ruinous cottages and huge chimney shafts, which look down on the little Bay of Gorey, as Gog and Magog look down on the visitors to the London Guildhall.

Leaving Gorey we had a good look at the rock called L'Etac de Sark with its satellites, and gave

ROCKS AT SOUTH END OF SARK.

them a wide berth, for their tooth-like appearance is not at all pleasant when but an inch of wood lies between one and a watery grave. L'Etac is the highest isolated rock round the island, rising nearly two hundred feet above low water.

To save time, instead of sweeping the bays we made a straight line, so as to pass between Point Derrible and La Couchée, and quickly arrived off what one may suppose the most picturesque spot in the Channel Isles—Creux Harbour, with its stumpy little breakwater pier and cave cutting which gives entrance to the island. The half-dozen fishermen on the quay gave us a cheer as we passed, in answer to a wave from my yellow cap.

On our right were the rocky islets, rising about one hundred feet above the sea, called La Burons, and I passed just in time to see a sheep fall with a plunge and splash into the sea, shot by a man in a boat. This appeared to be the local way of slaughtering the sheep which are put on the rocks to crop the sparse herbage which grows above high-water mark. After a fortnight among the rocks sheep will get so agile and surefooted, that a man has no chance with them in running or climbing, hence the rifle has to be employed to obtain mutton.

After passing Grand Moie (one hundred and seventeen feet)—there are no other rocks of any magnitude—so keeping well out I stripped and tumbled overboard, hanging now to the stern, and then swimming alongside, but never more than a yard away, for fear a current might part my boat and me. "Begum," of course, swam with me, and seemed to keep an eye on his master, for he seldom went far away from me. Whenever I looked round his dear old brown eyes were upon me, as if he would say, "How are you getting on, master?"

We rounded the northernmost point of Sark, a rock called Bec du Nez, about twelve a.m., and with a fair wind ran into Port Jument, where we hove to for dinner; then creeping round Point Moie de Mouton, anchored off the famous Gouilot caves, and took a sketch, but could not by reason of my compact enter them. This was very annoying, for I had heard so much about them and their wonderful pools and anemonæ. Disappointedly hauling in my anchor I steered for the Gouilot Pass, and like a fool nearly lost myself and craft. The distance between Moie de Gouilot and the island of Brechou is only about seventy yards, and as it was now past three o'clock, a swift tide was pouring pell-mell through the channel; this in my indolence I did not think of, and had like an ass taken a turn of the sheet round a cleat, and somehow got it jammed. Away went the "Yellow Boy," like a shot out of a gun, and as we passed through, a big puff of wind came round the end of Brechou, and nearly took the mast out before I could let go the sheet. Another two or three inches more and we must have capsized, and it was only due to the boat being rather heavily laden with cooking apparatus, gun, and cartridges, extra provisions, and the weight of "Begum" (eighty pounds), who was fortunately lying to windward, that we did not heel right over. As it was we were all afloat in each compartment, so I ran into the beautiful bay of Havre

Gosselin and anchored. It took an hour to bale out and sponge dry and put everything in order for the run home. After rightsiding, and when over my tea, I cast my eyes upon the beautiful precipitous vale which comes down from a height of about one hundred and fifty feet to the sandy shore. It was an exquisite sight in the full glow of the western sun, and would make a lovely theme for a canvas. It was an emerald valley, through the trees of which the sun glinted and made splendid contrasts of light and shade so beloved by the artist, while at the top of the vale, hung, or appeared to hang, half a dozen fishermen's cottages, such as the aforesaid artist frequently looks for in vain; but here they are, and perhaps my artistic friends may thank me for pointing out these delightful "bits" to them.

I lingered as long as prudence would allow at this enchanting spot, and crept along the lee of Brechou Island to get a peep at its harbour or port, and soon found it, facing due west, a snug little haven enough in calm weather; but the very thought of trying to get into it in a heavy sea was enough to make one shudder. A steep path leads up from the beach to a farmhouse, which stands high upon the island; it is the *only* habitation in the place.

This island is probably larger than Jethou, but being so near Havre Gosselin is not so lonely, as help may very quickly be summoned in case of accident or illness.

How I should have loved to pay the old farmer and his family a visit to compare notes with him; but it could not be, and even if I had seen him it is doubtful if I could have understood him, as doubtless he spoke Sarkoise French, and with that language I was totally unacquainted. Still, we might have had what the Indians call a "pow-wow," and fraternised to some extent if only by signs.

At a little past six away we steered for home, but with a head wind and rather choppy sea, so there was no help for it but to tack, which made a long trip of it; but to make it short to the reader we reached home about nine p.m., tired, wet, and hungry, for it began to drizzle at sundown. Still, I never enjoyed a trip better than this memorable one of about twenty-five miles, although I was glad after supper to lay my head down on my pillow (and dream it all over again).

At the risk of wearying my readers I must tell them of a trip I took round Guernsey about a month later.

"Begum" went with me, that was now a matter of course, for directly the boat was shoved off, he would jump in and take his seat as if he were pilot: there was no getting him out again.

Well provisioned and provided for casualties, we started at the somewhat late hour of six a.m., and in an hour made the land opposite St. Sampson's harbour, and peeped in on passing, so as to see the busy scene of granite trimming, breaking, and loading, which goes on here from sunrise to sunset all the year round. I could plainly hear the detonations as shots were fired in the quarries, and the dull rumble of the stone, as great masses of granite, which have been unmoved since the creation, were rent asunder and toppled into the quarry below. Vale Castle and Bordeaux harbour, where I anchored, look picturesque from whatever points they are seen, whether from land or sea, and two hours quickly glided by as I sketched the lovely little bits of scenery around me. My plan was to take about half an hour for each sketch, to get the general outline and feeling of color, so that on my return I had plenty to occupy me on a rainy day.

The next point of interest was a little rocky island just past Bordeaux, called Hommet Paradis, which is the scene of the death of Victor Hugo's hero, Gilliatt, as related in "The Toilers of the Sea." He creates a splendid hero, and in the last chapter makes him commit suicide in an impossible manner. He causes his hero to stand in the sea, so that the tide rises up to his feet, his knees, his waist, his shoulders, till, still watching the vessel which bears his love from him through his own stupid act, nothing but his head remains. Then the tide continues to rise, and as the vessel vanishes on the horizon, "the head of Gilliatt disappears. Nothing was visible now but the sea." Surely he might have left a lock of hair or a sigh to mark the spot where he disappeared. I have tried on even a very calm day to stand as Hugo's hero did, and let the tide rise around me, but find the thing an impossibility. The motion of the rising tide would lift one off their feet long before the water rose above their shoulders, and as to making the man stand *still* and drown, why the idea is ludicrous. But as Hugo created his hero, why should he not be allowed to destroy him as he likes? The book (except the last chapter) is an exquisite piece of word painting, but I always wish he had made a happy end of his hero. I felt this so much when I read it on Jethou (for the third or fourth time) that I actually re-wrote the last chapter for my own edification, and made Gilliatt marry Dérnchette willy-nilly, so that everything ended properly, and the lovers "lived happily ever after."

North Guernsey (called Parish) is very uninteresting, in fact, from the sea it looks a perfectly flat wilderness or desert, and I was glad when the "Yellow Boy" glided into the deep clear blue water of Grand Havre, where we moored for lunch.

Here an incident occurred which might have caused me to go ashore against my wish. While peppering some fish I was eating, the lid came off my little tin box, and the contents were strewn thickly on my food. Some of the condiment I scooped back into the box, and then gave a mighty puff to blow the rest off my plate, when, unluckily blowing against the wind, some of it blew into my eyes, causing me exquisite pain for some time, necessitating my rubbing them.

Had I remembered the Spanish proverb, "Never rub your eyes but with your elbows," I should have saved myself a lot of needless pain, for they became quite inflamed. I bathed them first in tepid water and afterwards in cold, and then sat down in the bottom of the boat with a wet handkerchief over them for an hour. This did them much good, but still they felt very hot and inflamed. I could only just see to pick my way among the shoals of rocks along this west coast, and consequently made very slow progress. Saline, Cobo, and Vazon Bays were all sailed slowly through, and very pretty they were; but it now dawned upon me that I should not see Jethou to-night, as it was already approaching the gloaming of the day. Lowering the sail I put out the sculls, and paddled back to a little inlet I had noticed near Cobo Bay, called Albecq Cove, a rocky little inlet, but nicely sheltered from the south-west wind, then gently blowing. Here I made all snug for the night; put on my kettle to boil water for tea, while with the sail I made a kind of awning to roof in the boat should it come on to rain, and made myself generally comfortable.

At nine p.m. I went to sleep, and at four a.m. was up again getting ready for a start. My eyes felt nearly well again, but still rather weak, so, stripping, I jumped overboard, and had a swim and dive, then dressed, and after a cup of coffee felt no more of the eye soreness.

Between Lihou Island and the shore I moored in shallow water to make a sketch of the remains of what are said to have once been a Priory, standing on the island, and which have since been used as a manufactory of iodine, although it is now discontinued. When my sketch was nearly completed, I became suddenly aware, by reason of the cessation of motion, that my craft was aground. Sure enough so it was, for the tide had left me on the causeway (laid bare at low tide), which serves as a means of communication with the shore for the family who occupy the only house on the eighteen-acre island. I jumped up and seized the oars, and pushed with main and utmost might, but the "Yellow Boy" refused to budge, and I was in a quandary. The tide would not float me for another three or four hours, so to wait would spoil my whole morning, and if I stepped overboard and pushed off, should I not be breaking my contract by landing? I sat down a few minutes and held council with myself, and came to the conclusion that to stand in a foot of water was not *landing*, so over I jumped, and by dint of a great deal of pushing, hauling, perspiring, and the use of interjections (not profane, for I never use a bad word), I got her off into deep water, and jumped in, resolving never to anchor again in fleet water with a falling tide.

From Lihou I made a bee-line to the Hanois lighthouse, which stands about a mile from the shore, and forcibly reminds one of the Longship Light off Land's End, Cornwall. I passed so close that the two men who were standing on the rocks with a tub between them doing their week's washing, asked me ashore; but I made a gurgling noise in my throat, and pointed to my ears and mouth as I passed on. I meant them to understand by this that I was a deaf mute, but they evidently took me for a lunatic, as I could hear by their remarks.

Rounding Pleinmont Point, upon which stands the dreary, solitary stone house mentioned so frequently in Hugo's "Toilers of the Sea," I caught the south breeze which was now blowing very fresh, and having a lea shore on my left, I had to give it rather a wide berth till I came to La Moye Point, where I turned into Petit Bo Bay for my mid-day meal, that being somewhat sheltered from the wind. It is a lovely little haven, and so I found Icart, Moulin-Huet, and Fermain Bays, with their Titanic surroundings.

While moored in Fermain Bay admiring the beautiful scene, the wooded slopes of the environing hills, the grand rocks, the pretty little semicircular stretch of yellow sandy beach, the puny little martello tower, and other items of interest, I discovered that while my surroundings were interesting *me*, that I was also interesting my surroundings, for I found I was gradually being surrounded by boats. These contained pleasure parties, to whom the fishermen had evidently told the story of my Crusoe life, and they were therefore anxious to get a near view of me and my curious craft, while "Begum" came in for his share of attention also.

Some of the people wished to speak to me, but I up anchor, and with my usual dumb appeal to my ears and mouth tried to get away, but there was so little wind under the great cliffs that my progress was very slow, so I had to sit, tiller and sheet in hand, while my tormentors said their say, to me and about me, in French, German, and English. One young lady, when she found I was dumb to her enquiries, made a confidant of "Begum," and told him how she would like to see over Crusoe's island, as she called Jethou, but all to no purpose, for, like his master, the dog was dumb also, though not deaf.

I should have bubbled over with pleasure to show the damsel my island and resources; but all I could do was to raise my yellow cap, and expand my mouth horizontally across my face, to signify my approval of her attention to *my dog!*

As the boat crept out from the headland of Fermain Bay my yellow sail began to draw, and very soon I left my pursuers behind. I had become so used to my queer yellow boat and its yellow sail and flag, that I had long ceased to see anything peculiar in it; but of course to other eyes my craft and its crew were a source of speculation and surprise. After this I never went near Guernsey again during the daytime.

I made a straight run for home now, but somehow felt rather melancholy, and could not get the young lady's face out of my mind. I felt somewhat depressed to think I was fleeing from my fellow-men, as if I had committed some grave offence and could not face them; but when once my foot touched Jethou's shore (about seven p.m.) my thoughts and melancholia vanished. There I was, home again, patting "Eddy's" back, and pulling his long ears, and feeding the pig, and milking the goat, getting ready my tea, and finally stretching my weary legs to take out the kinks, which a couple of days in an open boat will put into any man's limbs.

CHAPTER IX.

HARVEST OPERATIONS—EXPLORE LA CREUX DERRIBLE, AND NEARLY LOSE MY LIFE—CRUSOE ON CRUTCHES—AN EXTRAORDINARY DISCOVERY—KILL A GRAMPUS—OIL ON TROUBLED WATERS MAKE AN OVERFLOW PUMP.

AFTER my boating adventures I began to think it was high time I should spend a week or two ashore, looking after my crops and the estate generally.

It was now September, and my apples and pears were ripe, and so were the lovely mulberries. The giant tree was a sight to behold, with its bushels of red, purple, and blackish-ruby fruit. I might have gathered enough fruit and vegetables to have supplied a small community throughout the season, so prolific is the soil, and encouraging to vegetation the air.

My potatoes turned out remarkably well—free from blemish, and of good flavour. I must have had two or three tons, and went through the labour of digging them and picking up all the tiny ones, as if I expected or feared a famine. The pig's winter food was assured, at all events.

THE MAIN PATH OF THE ISLAND.

Long previous to this I had cut and gathered my hay crop, which was to form the chief sustenance for "Eddy," and the goat, "Corny," for the next five or six months. This I made into a neat stack close to the house, and thatched thickly with brakes, beside which I covered it with tarpaulin, and girded it about with old chain-cable to prevent its being blown away: also I guarded the base with a surrounding of wire-netting to preserve it from the rabbits.

The crop I took most pleasure in was the barley, which I looked upon as my legitimate harvest; the other crops seeming to be more like gardening than real harvest work. I cut every handful with a reaping hook, which took a long time; but as I had not a scythe this was my only way of cutting it down. True, the Channel Islands mode of harvesting the barley is to pull it up by the roots, a handful at a time, knocking the soil off the roots upon the toe of the boot; but this seemed to me such an un-English method that I would have nothing to do with it.

After it had lain to dry for three or four days I called "Eddy" and my solid-wheeled cart into requisition, and took it, load by load, down the rocky path to the store-house, where I placed it all safely away in the upper chamber. The pathway was so narrow in places that the deviation of a few inches would have caused donkey, load, and cart, to be precipitated scores of feet down the abrupt slope into the sea beneath. To avoid this catastrophe I had to take a pick-axe and shovel, and devote a whole day to widening it in parts, making this, the main path to the top of the island, nowhere less than four feet wide.

I rode home atop of the last load, and at my own door drank my own health, with three cheers for everything and everybody, to which "Flap," the gull gave a kind of croak, by way of approval to my sentiments.

While my harvest was in progress I met with an adventure which might have terminated the harvesting and my existence at the same time.

It was a boisterous day. I was tired of digging potatoes, for my back ached, and I wanted a rest. The Cotills being near the awful crater-like mouth of La Creux Derrible, I thought I would go and explore it, and find out in my own way, all about it; so, dropping my occupation, I wandered slowly down the zig-zag, bracken-hemmed path, lit my pipe, and prepared myself for laziness for an hour.

When I am lazy I like to be *thorough*. I cannot bear to be half at work and half at play; it is neither one thing nor another. So on this occasion I strolled quietly down the pathway, which zig-zags seven or eight times before it ends abruptly on the brow of a little cliff facing La Fauconnaire. I scrambled down the cliff, across the beach, and over the rocks which form a barrier to the entrance of the cavern leading to the Creux. I noticed that the tide allowed an entrance to be effected, so I climbed in over the gigantic boulders with which the floor of the black cavern is covered, and soon found myself standing on the pebbly floor of the chasm, looking up at its perpendicular sides, and admiring the various ferns, weeds, and flowers which grew in beauty from its many clefts and fissures. Then I saw something move in a hole near my feet, and found it to be a wounded rabbit, which had apparently fallen down the shaft from one of the little ledges a hundred and fifty feet above. The timid little fellow did not attempt to run away, so, picking him up, I examined him and discovered that both his fore legs were broken, and it quite hurt me to see the pitiful look he gave with his bright, prominent, gazelle-like eyes. I fondled the wounded animal, and looking upward intently, presently saw other little rodents hopping round little ledges near the top, which did not appear, from where I stood, to be so wide as their bodies; but there they were, and although I waited expectantly for a long time for a prospective dinner, no others fell upon me. I should have been afraid to shoot at them had I had my gun, for fear of detaching pieces of rock, which, falling from such a height, might have crushed my skull in.

Seeing it was hopeless to think of saving the poor little bunny's life, I gave him the "regulation stretch," and quieted him for ever. It seemed strange that I should have cared for this one's life, and would have saved it if I could, when I was daily trapping and shooting them in all directions.

I think it was his plaintive look that did it, or the consciousness that I was a superior being, and had his little life (to a certain extent) at my command, just as our Father above has mine; but anyway, in his wounded state I knew that death was his best friend. Looking round I at once realized what death meant —death in a terrible form—not to a rabbit, but *death to myself*—and for a moment I felt paralyzed; for there was the sea creeping in upon me, not ten yards away. The roof of the cavern through which I had to pass, did not appear far above the water at the outer mouth. As I gazed along the tunnel-like aperture the waves continually broke, sending spray to the roof, shutting out much of the daylight seaward, though from the opening above me the sunlit sky shed its light upon me.

Could I find a means of climbing up the perpendicular sides of my prison, if only a few feet? No, I could not see a spot where even a squirrel could ascend. What was to be done? The outlet was now filled to the roof with the incoming tide, which here has a rise of from twenty-five to thirty feet from low to high tide.

The sea reached my feet, and to my excited imagination felt like the fingers of death trying to clutch me. But I am not one to give up without a big struggle, and I made up my mind to attempt to swim round and round the opening, *like a rat in a pail*, if it came to the worst; but although I am a good swimmer, I doubted my ability to keep afloat for three or four hours, with a heavy sea pouring into the circular cavity, which would presently be filled with a whirlpool of seething, foaming water. I should be knocked and buffeted from side to side against the adamantine rocks till I was dead, then tossed and played with till the tide ran out and carried my body into the vast ocean beyond, as food for fishes. My friends would never hear of me again, and my animals on the island would starve till—yes, why not try?

My soliloquy was cut short by noticing a crag

project beyond the others about ten or twelve feet from the ground. Why could I not throw my doubled silk sash over it, and haul myself up? I would try.

The sea was now up to my knees, and was beginning to exert a rotary motion, which, as the tide rose, would increase in velocity. So off came my waist-sash, and after a few attempts it lodged over the boss of rock; then to strengthen it I twisted it like a double rope, and carefully hauled myself up it, hand over hand, till I grasped the protruding rock; but as it only jutted out a few inches there was no possibility of sitting upon it, so I gradually worked my way up by clutching at any inequalities in the surrounding rock till I got one knee upon it, and there I hung, with my fingers bent over a fissure like fish-hooks. How I envied the rabbits overhead, who occasionally dislodged the *detritus* of rock, which fell upon me. What would I not have given to be back on the ledges of the Cotills, digging potatoes! But there I was, like a rat in a trap, with no means of egress.

In a short time my fingers became cramped, and the sharp rock cut my knee to such an extent that the perspiration broke out clammily on my forehead, as I realised that in a few minutes I must loose my hold and drop into the whirling water beneath, unless I could find some other means of supporting myself. I looked about, and presently found a small hole for my right hand—one deep enough to get a fairly good hold upon—and putting my fingers into this, I gently let my left hand glide down the rock and bring up the sash on that side. This I placed in my mouth, gently changed hands and hauled up the right end of the sash, then, after many attempts, with my mouth and right hand I managed to tie a knot in it so as to form the sash into a short endless band. This I dropped down, and putting my foot in the loop, had a somewhat secure support.

LA CREUX DERKIBLE.

There I hung for about three hours, till the tide only left about two feet of water on the upper part of the floor of the cavern. When I attempted to descend I found I could not straighten my right leg because of the constant pressure for such a long time upon the knee-joint, so I waited till the cave floor was almost bare, and then let myself *fall* down as gently as possible. I was not hurt by the fall, but could not stand, as my knee would not allow itself to be straightened. I sat down for an hour till the tide allowed me to hop out in great pain. Oh, how glad I was to be out of that dreadful place; and even in my crippled state I rejoiced at my liberty! Upon getting to the foot of the Cotills cliff, I whistled for my faithful "Begum," but no "Begum" came, so I sat down and rested, and whistled, and whistled again, till presently away he came tumbling down the breech in the cliffs, to my great delight. After a bit I despatched him to fetch "Eddy," and while that worthy was on his way to my help, managed, with great exertion and risk, to scale the cliff. "Eddy" bore me up the zig-zag, and home by the lower path, and thankful indeed was I to get there.

I bathed my knee, and did all I could for it, but it was many days before I fully recovered the use of the limb; in fact, for three days I used a crutch, which helped me along famously. Fancy a Crusoe on crutches! After this adventure I made up my mind that I was not born to be drowned.

Now, a week after my Creux adventure another incident occurred which greatly influenced my career both as regards my stay on the island and my after life. This was a curious discovery I made quite by accident.

It happened to be a very wet morning when I rose, and looked as if it would continue all day, so I thought I would stay indoors and tidy up my dwelling. I soon prepared my breakfast, and sat down to enjoy it, and as I and my dog were discussing it, I could not help noticing the dilapidated state of the stained and ragged wall-paper. It had probably been on many years, and I recollected that somewhere among my stores I had about a dozen rolls of new paper, so I said to myself, "Why not strip the walls and re-paper the room?"

Good! I soon cleared the room, and with a pail of water and a brush began to soak the old paper and strip it off, when I found, to my surprise, that it was several layers thick—five at least—while underneath all was a kind of netting of some sort of linen-looking fabric. I surmised that this was to give a better adhesive power to the paste, as probably the walls might be damp, although they did not appear to be so. So I tore the various papers off the wall, till I clumsily dragged off a piece of the netting also. The netting came quite off in my hand; a circular piece, about eighteen inches across. I examined it to see what it really was, and to my amazement discovered it was a beautiful lace collar. What a curious way of putting a collar on I thought, and returned to the wall to see if it wore any other finery, and quickly discovered that the four walls were covered all over with lace of beautiful design. There were pieces of all shapes and sizes, and most of it of exquisite workmanship; so, packing it into a trunk with plenty of tobacco among it to keep away insects, I sealed it up, and stood it in a dry place for future consideration.

Even this curious find was not all I discovered, nor the most important, although at the time I made my second discovery I did not attach any value to it. It was this. When I came to the third side of the room, opposite the door, I came upon a sort of niche or cupboard, close up to the ceiling, which had no door, but simply a piece of lace tacked over the aperture, and then thickly papered over some seven or eight times.

The opening was about ten inches high, eight inches wide, by six inches deep, and in it stood two leathern drinking cups, capable of containing about a pint each. In the first I took down was a tiny vial and three gem rings, and in the second a small roll of paper, which upon unrolling I found to be about two feet long by four inches wide. Upon it, in very faded ink, was a long list of something in French. It looked like a very heavy washing bill, and I was about to throw it away when I reflected that it might tell something about the lace and the rings, so I rolled it up in a linen bandage, and put it and the other articles in my clothes box, so that some day I might get it deciphered.

All this made me very excited, and I am afraid my thoughts were more on my discoveries than upon my work, for the new paper was very badly put on the walls; it was not hung perpendicularly, and had several gaping joints, which annoyed me all the time I was on the island. But I had not paper enough to recover the walls, as I used the rest for my bedchamber; therefore it remained, a lasting memorial of my slovenliness and bad workmanship.

About this time I shot a curious specimen—too large for stuffing—a grampus. I was in my boat one day fishing for whiting, when I heard a peculiar noise behind me, and looking round, saw a huge monster rise from the sea about a hundred yards off, and make straight for me. Before getting to the boat he dived again and again, when I saw that it was apparently a young whale. Instinctively I clutched my gun, and as the monster dived within a dozen yards of my boat I watched its rising; up he came, not twenty feet away, whereupon I let him have both barrels at the back of his head, and to my surprise he immediately turned over, belly upward, gave a shudder, and was dead. I took my prize in tow, and found on landing that it was upwards of ten feet long, and must have weighed several hundredweight, for out of the water it was perfectly unmanageable. I had to yoke "Eddy" and myself together, and drag the monster above high water-mark, till I decided what to do with it.

In the morning I took off the skin, which would have made excellent leather, but I had no means of tanning it, so was jettisoned. Beneath the skin was a thick layer of blubber, and this I flayed off, making myself in a pretty pickle, and soon had a large pile of this reeking adipose deposit. Then I brought my copper on the beach, as it was a portable one, and lighting a fire I "tryed," or boiled my blubber down and had several gallons to bottle by the end of the day.

The flesh, I believe, is eatable, but it looked so dark and rich that I was afraid to cook a piece and try it. Grampus is, no doubt, all very well for shipwrecked mariners, but as I had plenty of other food the carcase followed the skin into the sea. As it glided into the rough water the oil exuded, and made a large patch of calm water as smooth as a mill-pond.

This gave me a splendid idea for using the oil. For the future I would always take some with me on my boating expeditions! I did, and put it in a bottle which I kept near the bows, and whenever I got into difficulties near rocks or in a rough sea I could command a calm. This power I used on many occasions, and with invariable success. For instance, if my lines got foul in a choppy sea, I could make the sea calm, and get my gear out of tangle capitally, which, with the pitching of my craft and the "send" of the following waves, would have otherwise been a nearly hopeless task. Another use I put the oil to was to pour some on my fish pond and bring the surface to a perfect calm; then I could study my fish as well as if they were simply under a sheet of glass, while by lying flat down on the margin of the pool, with my face near the water, I could see even the most minute object on the bottom. Looking into this pool was to me like looking into another world. Once when very intent upon the doings of some spider-crabs, the rock upon which I leaned my chest and hands gave way beneath my weight, and I was immediately transformed into a fish, or at any rate, for some moments I was an occupant of the same element and abode as the fish; but I soon scrambled out without even a crab or lobster taking the opportunity of tweaking my nose.

To keep up my supply of oil I was continually on the look out for grampuses or porpoises; but I did not see another of the former, although plenty of the latter were to be seen at times—generally out of range. Two I shot, but I believe when hit they sink. Anyway I did not see either of them again, although the water was coloured with blood, shewing that my aim had been true. I doubly wished to get a porpoise, for the sake of its oil, and also to cut a steak and try its flavour, as I have heard that in some of the ports on the eastern seaboard of the United States, boats are fitted out to capture young porpoises for the hotels, as porpoise calf is considered a delicacy. If cod liver oil is good for consumptives, why not porpoise cutlets?

How I would have liked to place a porpoise in my fish pond! What a rumpus he would have caused? I might have seen him then in his habit as he lived.

My bucket pump frequently took it into its head to go on strike; that is, it would work when it pleased, and be idle if it wished; so I had to supplement it with another kind of apparatus. This contrivance was by using a nine-foot length of four-inch iron piping, which I found in the boat-store, and which had probably belonged to some vessel as the barrel of a pump, or something of the kind. To this I fitted a long wooden piston, having a wooden disk on the end, through which I cut a circular hole, and fitted over it a leathern valve. When I pushed this piston down into the water the valve would open and the water would enter the barrel, and when I drew the piston up the valve would close and draw the water to the mouth of the pipe, where it poured out of a hole a few inches from the top into a wooden trough, which conveyed it into the pool. This meant hard manual labour; but as I only had to use it about once a week it was exercise for me, and I enjoyed it. So did the fish, for they would come to the new water in numbers, either because of the food contained in the water, or because of its coolness in the hot weather, or some other reason that I am not scientist enough to fathom.

My pond was my place of meditation, and often I would dream a couple of hours away, thinking of home and those dear to me. I was like Adam, and sometimes sadly sighed for my Eve; but Eve, otherwise Priscilla, was hundreds of miles away; so I sighed and yawned, and made myself very content with my dog and gun, and other belongings.

CHAPTER X.

A STORM AND A WRECK—THE CASTAWAY—DEAD—
A NIGHT OF HORROR—THE BOATHOUSE DES-
TROYED—A BURIAL AT SEA.

INTER was now rapidly approaching, but before its advent something of a very grave nature happened.

It had been a very blustering day, with occasional showers of sleet, when about four p.m. I found myself standing by the watch-house, holding my hat on; the sun fast setting in a very angry-looking sky.

Evidently a storm was brewing, so I hauled my saucy little "Yellow Boy" high above high-water line, and made everything snug before I went indoors just after darkness had fallen all around. I felt uncomfortable somehow, but could not tell why; but when the time for bed came, and the wind was howling round the house as if it meant to cast it bodily into the sea, I did not for some reason care to turn in; so replenishing my lamp I sat down to read, but the wind shook the casements so roughly that I had to give it up. About midnight, although it was late in the autumn, a flash of lightning lit up the room and startled me; in a few seconds the thunder began to roll, but a long way off.

I sat waiting for another flash, and presently it came, this time with the thunder much nearer. A little while and another more vivid flash, with the thunder close to its heels, upon which I started up on the impulse of the moment and donned my oil-skin suit and sou'wester and sallied out into the night; why I knew not. At first the night was pitch dark, but a flash of brilliant lightning seemed to light up the whole island, while at the same time came a crash of thunder, such as I hope never to hear the like of again. It was as if the whole of the granite island had been shivered to atoms by some awful volcanic crash; in fact, I thought it was an earthquake. It only lasted a few seconds, but it seemed to literally paralyze me; so much so, that I thought I should have fallen. Other flashes succeeded, one of them striking a granite block, which it shivered to pieces, although it weighed many tons, and in the shock appeared itself to be broken; that is, it seemed like the first stroke of a smith's hammer upon a red hot piece of iron, when the sparks fly off in every direction. I dare not go along that path, although it was now probably the safest; but as I went towards the beach I could see the lightning run among the wet rocks like phosphorus.

As I stood by the watch-house I fancied I could detect human voices crying for aid, but put it down to my imagination, till I saw, to my horror, not a hundred yards from the shore, a French Chasse-maré, or fishing boat, driving straight for the rocks. I shouted, but the noise of the breaking sea rendered it inaudible five yards off against such a wind. Two of her three masts were gone, and by the next flash I could distinguish several men crouching by the bulwarks, and one at the tiller. Then came a sudden lurch and a dead stop, a tremendous sea crashed on deck, and I knew she had struck the rocks on the beach not fifty yards from where I stood.

Heaven help them, for no earthly power could. I was helpless to render the slightest assistance. I could only pray, and that I did fervently. Doubtless the men would jump into the sea, with the very remote chance of being thrown ashore alive, but that was very improbable.

Still, there *was* a chance, and I went along the beach, as far as the nature of the rocky shore would allow me, up and down, up and down, like a dog on a race course, till at last, among a lot of cordage and fishing gear, I thought I espied a man cast ashore, and so it was. He was entangled in the mass of wreckage, and appeared dead. As I thought a spark of life might still remain, I tried to disengage him, but try as I would I could not disentangle his legs, so had recourse to my knife to cut away the ropes which held him so fast. This I found a long process, but at length I freed the poor fellow, and carried, or rather half dragged him to the shelter of some rocks, and tried to revive him. His heart still beat, so I ran to the house and got a bundle of straw and some brandy. With the straw I made him a kind of bed, as he was a big man, and the pathway too steep for me to carry him up, and pouring some brandy into his mouth as he lay back I succeeded in causing him to open his eyes, after about twenty minutes. I chafed his hands and did all I could for him, and then ran back to procure more comforts. When I returned he appeared much better; but although he looked at me he appeared unable to speak, although he made a curious unintelligible noise, such as one hears a dumb man make when he wishes to call a person's attention. I noticed that blood was oozing from the corners of his mouth, and signed to him to open it, when, to my horror, I perceived that he had bitten his tongue completely off; hence his inability to articulate. I then proceeded to examine him all over, but when I touched his body he gave great groans, so that I would fain have left him alone, had I not considered it my duty to act the Good Samaritan to him.

I tried to persuade him by signs to rise, that I might support him to the house, but he shook his head and groaned again, when it occurred to me that his legs might be injured, and this I found to be but too true; both his thighs were broken. Then an idea came happily to my mind, I would fetch my donkey and cart, and so endeavour to get him by a circuitous route to the house and put him to bed.

Away I went and harnessed my faithful servant to his wonderful cart, and was back again in about twenty minutes; but that short period had bereft me of my patient, for when I bent over him to see if he were better, I found he was again senseless. Taking up the lantern so that it shed its full light on his face, I at once saw, to my consternation, that he was dead. His eyes were wide open, and his teeth clenched in such a ghastly manner as to make me, for a brief time, tremble with horror to think I was thus left alone with a corpse.

I threw a handful of straw over the awful countenance, and went home in an unutterable frame of mind, as to me death has a most unnerving effect. I laid down on my bed, after taking off my wet oil skins; but sleep would not give me the oblivion I so craved till dawn. Sometimes I dozed off, but only to dream horribly, so that I would awake in a great perspiration, and with my nerves thoroughly unstrung, I would start to my feet and gaze round the room, as if I expected some dread visitor. It was an awful night for me.

About four o'clock in the morning I had just dozed off again, when a loud gust of wind gave my window an extra hard rattle, which woke me. I laid quite still, but presently heard a curious shuffling outside my door, which made me sit upright upon my bed, with my eyes starting from my head, and riveted upon the door, which gradually opened with a peculiar sliding noise, little by little, in jerks, and as it did so I could feel my hair move on my head, as if trying to stand on end with horror, but as it was very long it could only move in locks like writhing eels. Little by little the door opened, and I expected to see my black-bearded dead giant, with the awful face enter. I looked instinctively near the top of the door for the face to show itself; but such an awful visitant I was not doomed to see, though in his place, and much nearer the floor, appeared a black head surmounted by a pair of pointed horns. My eyes seemed as if they

TOO LATE!

would fly from their sockets at this sight, but only for a minute, for a body followed the head, which was perfectly familiar to me—*it was my goat.*

I dropped upon my bed, overcome by the sudden change from horror to joy, and laid there for some minutes, till the faithful Nanny came and licked my ear and brought me back to consciousness again.

I afterward accounted for her unexpected visit by surmising that the wind must have blown open the outer door and let her into the passage, as I had never fastened the doors, although the outer ones were provided with bolts. Then Miss Nanny must have pushed open the door of my room with a series of prods with her nose, and as she did so the old rug, which I always threw at the bottom of the door to keep out the draught, was gradually forced back till she had made sufficient space for the admission of her body.

Oh, the horrors of that night! Shall I ever forget them? No, not if I live to the age of Noah, who ran his grandfather, Methuselah, very close in the race of years.

Day *did* dawn at last, and putting out my lamp I slept soundly for several hours; in fact, when I awoke it was mid-day, and the sun shining down pleasantly from a blue and cloudless sky.

I breakfasted, fed my animals, and then—then! *What of the dead man lying on the beach?* I shuddered at the mere idea of going near the poor fellow. I dreaded gazing upon that face again—it *must* be done, still it need not be done *just* yet. I would take a walk round the island and see if the storm had thrown up anything else upon the shore, and give myself time to think what I should do with the dead Frenchman. I would walk the reverse way round to that which I usually did; that is to go round past the boathouse, and thus along the east shore. This I did so that I might make the tour of the island before seeing the dreadful man again.

Gun on shoulder, and dog at heel, I started slowly along, but had not gone more than two hundred yards —in fact, had only just got in sight of the boathouse— when I was startled by its changed appearance. The roof was completely gone, and so were huge masses of the walls, the stones of which were scattered thickly about the pathway along which I was walking. I was so excited by the curious appearance that I actually ran towards the building, as if the remaining portion had made up its mind to take its flight after the part which was missing.

When I arrived at the ruins I soon discerned what had taken place. The lightning had struck it last night, and what felt to me like an earthquake was the explosion of my large cask of gunpowder. The boathouse was a complete ruin, and the ruin involved the loss of many things of great value to me, among them being my canoe, most of my lamp oil, paints, and above all, tools.

I was like the prophet Jeremiah weeping over Jerusalem, for I sat down on a rock, and viewing the desolation around me, wept also. Then I dried my wet cheeks, and there and then set about clearing the ruin. But it was a great task, and would take several days before I could clear the debris and recover such goods and chattels as were not totally destroyed. I dug, I heaved over great masses of granite wall which had been tumbled inward and outward by the explosion, I sawed through beams and hacked through rafters with an axe, but my thoughts were not altogether with my work.

Every man has a skeleton in his cupboard, but I had more; I had a whole carcase lying near my house, and this occupied my mind as much as my labour. As I thought of it, so the harder I worked, but to no purpose, and presently, for a spell of breathing, I sat down, axe in hand, upon a beam, and resolved to decide there and then what to do.

During the daylight I did not so much mind my dread visitor, but it was the approaching night I did not like. Why are we so much more in fear of unseen things at night than during the day? Whence comes the spell of dread that night brings beneath its black wing? Does darkness affect the nerves of a blind man as it does that of one with his full visual powers? I think not. Probably day and night are but as one to the blind. Then why does darkness bring a certain awe to ordinary mortals?

But to resume the thread of my narrative.

It appeared to me that there were three courses open to me. I could fire the cannon (I had a few pounds of powder in the store near the house) and summon aid; I could dig a grave and bury the body; or I could hitch on my donkey and drag it down to the water at low tide, and let it be washed whithersoever the sea should take it.

I did not like either of these plans. If I fired the

cannon it would bring a posse of curious, prying people to the island, and probably I should be taken away to St. Peter Port upon a coroner's quest. If I buried the man I should always shun that part of the island, and should have a constant memorial of my "night of horror" to depress me; while if I committed the body to the waves I should for ever have it on my conscience that I refused burial to a christian.

Then I thought, why not at dawn in the morning tow the body to Herm, and drag it ashore on the rocks opposite the labourers' cottages, as if it had been flung there by the waves; but a high sea was running, and to my craft the passage of the Percée was impossible, for the current running through it would have swept me away, so that with a weight towing astern I should never have reached Herm, not even if I had taken the corpse as a passenger inside my boat. I lit my pipe to conjure up fresh inspiration, and the charm worked, for I got an idea which seemed to me to fulfil all my requirements from a religious point of view, and it also appeared practicable.

Being a sailor, my idea was to give the poor fellow a sailor's funeral, and *bury him myself at sea;* and if the sea were not too rough it should take place this very night. It wanted yet an hour of dusk, and I would commence my preparations at once. Having formed my plan, and looked calmly upon my undertaking as one that was a *duty* for a christian man to perform, the fear in a great measure seemed to leave me.

I hauled down my boat, with "Eddy's" help, to high-water mark, and then went, with as bold a mien as I could muster, to the poor man's side; nerving myself with a prayer I lifted the straw from his face, and was pleased to find that the features had assumed their normal aspect, in fact but for the eyes being partly opened, he looked as if he were asleep. This was a great relief to me, and I now felt firm for the task I had undertaken. I got the body on the cart by great exertion, and transported it to the boat, where I laid it across amidships on two planks and tied a huge rock to each ankle; then, having prepared everything by the time night set in, I left the boat, as I found the tide would not float her away, and went home.

I thought if I waited another four or five hours the swell of the sea would run down with the tide and become calm enough for me to venture out upon my mission. I therefore had a substantial meal, and lay down on my bed to rest, as I was very tired with my day's work and my previous sleepless night.

When I awoke I found that it was past eleven p m., but on looking out discovered that it was a fine night, though very dark. The sea had greatly quieted down, so taking my lantern and dog, I blundered along down the rocky path with "Eddy" at my heels, till I came to the boat of which I was presently to become the Charon.

With "Eddy's" help the boat was safely, though riskily launched, as my passenger made it very top heavy. Seeing this, I caught "Begum" up and tossed him overboard, so that he might swim ashore again, which I daresay he thought a great liberty and very unkind, but it was a necessity.

Away into the darkness of the night I steered my little bark, among the big hills and vales of the pathless deep. When I had gone as far as I judged it prudent to venture, I thought I would drop anchor and down sail, and accordingly hove the anchor overboard; but somehow the sail would not descend. I had therefore to climb over my passenger and go to the foot of the mast with the lantern to see what was amiss. I found the halyard had jammed in the sheave, and in trying to release it, as the boat slid down the side of a great black wave, she gave a tremendous lurch, and I thought was about to capsize, but she righted quickly as the yard came down on my head by the run. I gathered in the canvas and turned round to see how I could make room for the yard to lie safely when, presto, the dead man was gone! It certainly made my heart give a big thump, but a moment's reflection shewed me that the rolling of my boat had caused the body to shoot off the boards, feet downward, thus saving me the trouble of having to tip it off the planks.

The boat was now in good trim, and I had no fear for her safety nor my own, so placing the lantern on the floor, I sat down and read by its uncertain light the stirring service for the "Burial of those who die at Sea." Fervently I said those prayers as the salt spray, mingling with my tears, ran down my face, and when I pronounced the words, "I therefore commit his body to the deep," I looked around fearfully, as if the man might still be near me, but I saw him no more.

The bell of St. Peter's struck twelve o'clock just as

the service was finished, sounding as I had never heard it sound before—so solemn and full of meaning as it tolled out in the still midnight air.

I pulled back with great effort, by reason of the heavy roll of the sea, and landed by the ruined boathouse, with great risk of losing both myself and boat. When safely ashore at last I was thankful to have accomplished my dread mission without accident. As I hauled my boat up I felt as if a tremendous weight had been lifted from my shoulders, and was quite happy again; probably at having acted the Good Samaritan to a man who, like the one in the Bible, was not of the same country or creed as myself.

CHAPTER XI.

CLIMATE IN WINTER—VISION OF MY FATHER—A WARNING VOICE—SUPERNATURAL MANIFESTATIONS—THE FALLING ROCK—MY LIFE SAVED BY MY DOG.

WINTER was now come, but a very different atmosphere prevailed to what I had been used to in my Norfolk home. There I was accustomed to see the broads and rivers frozen over, and the means of communication by boat between the various rivers completely stopped. There we dreaded the marrow-piercing north-east wind which, coming straight across the cold North Sea from ice-bound Norway and the frozen Baltic, caused everything, animal and vegetable, to be cut and chilled, so that frequently both man and plant succumbed to its penetrating rigour; but here the north or east wind is not nearly such a dreaded visitor, and it is only on exceptional days that its biting power is felt.

There nothing seemed to grow during the winter, all vegetation slumbered, sometimes never to awaken; here in mid winter the primrose and violet were in full bloom, and on New Year's Day I gathered quite a posy of garden flowers, including roses and other fragrant flowers.

Snow fell on two or three occasions, but the bright sun dissipated it very quickly, and the frosts were not at all severe; in fact, were only of occasional occurrence. These frosts are only severe enough to hurt one class of persons, and that is the gardeners, who dread a frost coming after the blossoms are set on the trees. The climate being so mild the blossom buds burst at a very early period, so that a late frost coming nips them, then good-bye to the fruit.

Frequently potatoes are here being eaten before the green tops are above ground in England, which is another proof of the mildness of the climate. No doubt this mildness and equability of temperature is due in a great measure to the influence of the Gulf Stream, which keeps the surrounding sea at an even temperature; the sea in turn tempering the wind, keeps the thermometer very level.

There is usually a very mild fortnight towards the end of October, which the natives call "La petite éte;" it appears like a return of summer, and is greatly enjoyed by everyone as the last of the really warm weather.

In the matter of sunshine England cannot be compared with these islands, for taking our much-favoured Devonshire, and comparing the hours of sunshine for December, January, and February, I find that in the Channel Islands the sun shews its face just double the number of hours that it does in fertile Devon.

In my garden on January 25th I had peas a foot above ground. How I should have liked to shew my

A GHOSTLY VISITANT.

father these, he would scarcely have believed his eyes, for April 25th in Norfolk, would not have produced anything much more forward.

Now, having mentioned my father, I must tell a curious incident which happened concerning him upon the last day of January. About eight o'clock in the evening I was sitting finishing a sketch of Creviçhon, with my dog lying asleep near the fire, when he suddenly half raised himself, and looking towards the other end of the room commenced to whine.

I followed his eyes, and there to my astonishment sat my father. He sat on a stool facing me, with his leg, which was enveloped in a huge covering, upon another stool. His right hand rested upon the covered leg, while his left was placed upon his heart. As the dog whined he looked straight at me, and in his well-known voice said,

"It's all right, Harry, my boy, but it *was* a shake!"

I stood up to rush to him, but as I rose he melted away, leaving nothing but the two empty seats. I was staggered, but calm immediately, for I had read of things of this kind before, and concluded that my father had met with some accident, and had thus by some unknown means communicated with me in spirit.

I knew nothing of the why or wherefore of this wonderful means of communication between two persons, but judged that in this case it happened in this wise. My father had met with a severe accident, which he was probably afraid might have had a fatal termination, that his thoughts were intent upon me, his absent son. As he intently thought of me, and how he should like to speak to me, he may have actually spoken the words to himself, which by some unknown means I heard apparently fall from his own lips, and in his very voice.

The words assured me of his safety, and therefore beyond taking a note of the day and the hour, I did not trouble myself much more about the curious incident.

While on this subject of the apparently supernatural, I will mention one or two other inexplicable things which occurred to me during my residence on Jethou.

One night in autumn I could not sleep, so towards dawn got up and dressed myself, as I had frequently done before, and took a walk round the island, a distance of over a mile. This proceeding always had the effect of giving me the desired sleep upon my again wooing Morpheus. On this particular night my mind was filled with the question, "How can I keep my fish pond always replenished with sea water?" and as I wandered on in the dark, knowing the path so well, I was concocting a new pumping device, when my steps were suddenly arrested by the word "Harry!" pronounced gently but plainly just behind me. This woke me abruptly from my reverie, and I turned round quickly, but could see nothing but my faithful dog at my heels. "Strange, very strange indeed," I thought, and was about to resume my walk, but there, not four steps away, was the yawning abyss of La Creux Derrible, into which I should have walked in another second, and been dashed to pieces on

K

the rocks below. My life was saved, but by what? Was it a spirit voice or some night bird that in my abstraction I fancied pronounced my name?* Some will say the latter, but I must maintain that it was a curious thing that this should happen at precisely the correct instant, just in time to save me from a violent death. It *was* a voice, for I recognized it as that of my own love, Priscilla, who was at the moment two or three hundred miles away. But how could *she* know of my danger?

It may strike the reader as strange, and it is *strange*, I will allow; but on another occasion my life was saved in a remarkable manner. One afternoon late in the winter, after a heavy fall of rain, I was sitting near the brink of the granite cliff on the west side of the island, making a sketch of some rock masses in the glow of the ruddy setting sun, when "Begum" became suddenly restive, and rubbed several times with his head against my leg, looking up into my eyes at intervals. Then he would walk away, looking round as if wanting me to follow and see something (a proceeding he had often done before); but being busy I did not give way to his solicitations, and went on working. This did not

---

* I am aware that these things are but trifles to the Theosophists and Esoteric Buddhists, who profess to project their astral bodies, and play many other hocus pocus tricks of transmitting voices and articles to immense distances. They may therefore be able to explain these phenomena, I cannot; still I have the belief that there is some spirit-force which can and does act as a medium between distant persons who are in sympathy with each other.

please him, for he now took hold of my coat sleeve, and gave me a tug, with his eyes at the same time fixed on mine; so, to oblige him, I rose, and went after him to see what wonder he had to shew me. Contrary to his usual custom he appeared to have nothing for me to see, but seemed pleased to have me follow him, shewing his joy by wagging his tail, as if he would wriggle his body in two, and looking up into my face over his shoulder to shew his pleasure. As I had nearly finished my sketch I thought I would humour him, and avoid taking cold by sitting too long in the cool atmosphere among the damp rocks. With this thought in my mind I turned round to fetch my colours and sketch, when suddenly near the top of the island a large block of granite, about the size of a thirty-six gallon barrel became detached, and commenced a downward career, crashing all before it in its course. I paused and watched it, waiting to see it bury itself with a mighty splash in the sea.

It descended in leaps and bounds with increasing velocity, till, with a final rise it launched itself upon the very stone on which I was sitting a minute before, and with a sharp crash broke it completely in two, hurling the pieces and itself the next instant into the sea!

My sketch went with the rocky seat, and but for the intervention of my dog I should have been *killed* first and drowned *afterwards*. My colours, lying on the ground a foot away, were uninjured.

What is the interpretation of this? It might be said that the previous heavy rains had loosened the rock, and the warm sunshine having swelled the mass or the earth beneath, had overbalanced it, and thus nearly brought about a catastrophe. But what of the dog's warning? It was *strange*, that is all the solution I can give. As a Norfolk labourer once said to me when I was pumping him upon the subject of superstition,

"Master, there's more things about than we knows of about both by day and night."

Perhaps there are, and if they are *things* of *good*, so much the better. We know of hypnotism, psychic force, spiritualism, thought reading, and other occult sciences which appear to produce nothing very grand as results for *good*, but who shall say there is not some "Guiding Good" which can (even against our wills) warn us, or sway our minds in a given direction or in some way influence our movements, by means *outside ourselves?*

Sometimes after dark, with a half gale blowing, I have fancied all kinds of things were about, of which the eye or ear might get indistinct glimpses, and with the wind sighing and moaning among the trees and rocks and my solitary life also taken into consideration, was this to be wondered at.

Solitude gives latitude for an imaginative mind to expand itself, and for one shut up by himself as I was, trifles are frequently made prominent, simply because there is nothing greater to attract one's attention and thought.

The wind sweeping among the rocks in a gale, will at times, form at it were, notes or peculiar noises, which will, with other sounds of rustling branches, the cry of wild fowl and the beat of the sea on the shore, all taking place concurrently, cause the listener to imagine he hears voices. Again, who has not, when walking by a noisy babbling brook, where it falls among rocks and other impediments in a quiet place, heard as he has thought voices as of persons conversing at a distance? Many trout-fishers will have heard these sounds, and know the reason of their being heard; they can fully explain the cause, but I doubt if they could explain the curious experiences related in this chapter.

CHAPTER XII.

A FAIRY POOL—WONDERS OF THE DEEP—PORTRAIT OF A POET—THE CAVE OF FAUCONNAIRE—A LETTER FROM HOME AND MY ANSWER TO IT.

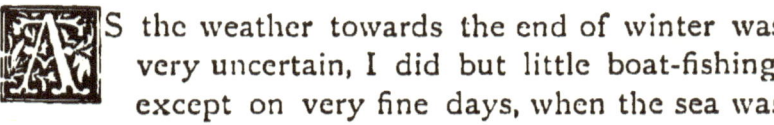

AS the weather towards the end of winter was very uncertain, I did but little boat-fishing, except on very fine days, when the sea was fairly calm, and I had a longing for a certain kind of fish. At such times I would embark for an hour or two, and rarely came home empty-handed.

Crabs and lobsters I soon got tired of, and I think most people who could eat their fill of them for the mere catching would do the same; but a nice sole or slice of turbot takes a long time to satiate one's appetite.

Although little could be done in the garden or field during the winter days I was never idle; that is, I never indulged in lying in bed or letting the time slip dreamily by, so as to induce the belief that I was enjoying myself. No, that would not suit me at all, for my disposition was to be ever on the go—seeing, hearing, or trying to learn something. Thus I knew almost every rock and cranny round the island, as I was always poking and ogling into odd crannies and pools to see what I could discover. Among my favourite places was the Fauconnaire, which being surrounded at every tide, was always having fresh life and vegetation brought to it by the ever-moving sea.

There were many pools and wonderful little caves round this curious, conical island, of which I knew, and into whose recesses I loved to pry; and although I visited them frequently they seemed ever new to me.

There was, facing due east, a large mass of rock near the foot of the Fauconnaire, upon which I often sat on a calm day, looking down into the mysteries of the sea. The water was so wonderfully clear, that at a depth of twenty feet I could see every pebble and bunch of weed as plainly as if only a sheet of glass hid them from view. This was to me very remarkable, as on the sandy east coast of England, an object two or three feet beneath the surface is hidden from the eye by the discolouration of the water, caused by the sand and soft clay cliffs. Here I could look down at one of the most lovely gardens the eye of man ever rested upon.

It was a wonderfully diversified collection of marine plants of all sizes, shapes, and colours; in fact, a perfect marine paradise. The colours embraced every hue of green, from the pale tint of a cut cucumber to the darkest shade of bronze, merging upon blackness. The yellow plants embraced every tint of yellow and orange imaginable, while the pinks ran the whole gamut of shades of that colour.

The forms and sizes of this enchanting garden of

flowers without blossom were as varied as the colours. On the rocky slopes adhered tiny anemonæ; lower down were other bushy weeds growing in all forms and positions, while further away in the deeper water rose up great feathery fronds and waving arms, like the tentacles of some giant octopus feeling for its prey. This bed of snake-like brown arms was a weird spot, which only wanted a mermaid or two to make it complete; but I, as a *mere man*, could only complete the picture by magnifying in my mind's eye the innumerable fishes which swam in and out among the luxuriance of marine vegetation, so as to fancy them mermaidens, and thus people this wonderful water palace.

The fish sometimes came along in shoals, principally the spotted rock-fish, which seemed to be painted by nature to resemble the colours of the surrounding rocks, stones, and sea-weed. Sometimes they would appear singly, swimming hurriedly, just giving the leaves a pat with their tails, as if closing the door behind them. These seemed to be messengers, for presently others of a larger size would come along more leisurely, as if to clear the way, and in a short time would appear quite a shoal of these beautiful fish of all sizes, forming a procession, as if they had some kind of carnival or festival afoot, and were making the most of the day.

What a spot for a poet to muse in! How he could roll his azure eyes and comb out his locks with his lily-white taper fingers, and gaze into space for a word to rhyme! How he would wrinkle his lofty brow, compress his cupidon upper lip, and unloose his *negligé* necktie, to give room for his bosom to swell with pride at the enchanting poem which would, at the picture before him, be sure to flow from the tip of his pretty little golden stylographic pen! At least this is how I fancy a poet must act, but never having seen one of those wonderful beings at work, I have, like the said poet, to get my picture from the source of some of his best work—the imagination.

But a truce to badinage. True poetry is not a thing to laugh at and disdain, for it is the salt of life, which makes existence endurable, and gives a savour to our worldly toil.

Pierce, a modern poet, hits off the shores of Jethou capitally, thus:

> "Lucent wave!
> Flash in sparkling bells
> On the coloured stones and tiny shells;
> With low music lave
> Sheltering rock,
> Flood the glassy pool,
> Sway the foliage 'neath its crystal cool,
> Wake with gentle shock
> The anemonæ,
> That like some lovely flower
> Petals opening 'neath the sunlight's power,
> Its beauty spreads to thee."

At low tide—or rather, at half tide—may be seen a huge square-headed fissure or cave quite through a portion of La Fauconnaire. Its sides are walls of granite, and the roof is also of that stone, from ten to twelve feet high on the average, but much more in parts. Although daylight is admitted at each end of this tunnel it is somewhat gloomy in the centre, which perhaps adds to its charms, as objects are seen less clearly, thus giving more scope to the imagination, of which daylight is frequently a great destroyer. Semi-gloom causes one to speculate upon things which, seen in the broad glare of day, have nothing of mystery or wonder about them; they are but too evident to the eye. A grammar-school education does not permit of great descriptive flights, or this cavern would be for me an exquisite theme upon which to write a chapter on fairyland.

The walls of this vaulted chamber sparkled from the constant dripping of water, which appeared to ooze from the sides and roof as the tide went down; but what appeared most noticeable was the pink hue of these walls, which upon closer inspection appeared to be lined with a kind of coral, or some such substance, while here and there from roof and walls depended most lovely fern-like sea-weed, whose long fronds waved gracefully in the grateful breeze which came in from the south end in puffs, just enough to stir the glorious pool of water covering the whole floor of the cave. The chamber is not very wide, probably not more than from four to five feet, so that the pool on the floor forms a miniature lake of surpassing beauty, some forty or fifty feet long, and from one to two feet deep; but the contents and the arrangement of that pool who shall describe? In this small space may be found animal and vegetable life of all kinds, anemonæ, lovely weeds, zoophytes, curious fish, sponges, shells, coral, and a hundred other things, all in such perfection and orderly wildness that no artificial aquarium can ever hope to present, for they are made by hands, and can never vie with Nature in the formation of the wild and picturesque aspect of these rocky pools.

As the sea filled this cave at every tide there was always something new for me to admire whenever I made a visit, and my only regret was that I could not take it home with me if I should be spared to see Norfolk again.

Now to proceed a little further with my narrative.

Christmas was a time which I knew not how to fill up. I wanted to be jolly and to make some festive difference in the usual routine of my daily life and fare, but with no companion I found it a very difficult task, even to make myself believe it really was Christmas time.

I made a plum pudding which had scarcely the consistence to hang together when I rolled it out of the cloth; but that mattered little, as a broken pudding required less muscular activity for the jaws. The main point was the flavour; it was not at all bad. Tinned beef, potatoes, tomatoes, a cauliflower, a rabbit pie, walnuts, and apples formed my Christmas dinner, which was washed down by a bottle of Bass I had reserved as a special Christmas treat. I drank the health of my absent friends, and even gave three cheers for the King of Jethou—myself.

To make the season appear as Christmassy as possible I cudgelled my brain for a whole week, and composed what I am pleased to call

A CHRISTMAS CAROL.*

In olden time a child was born
    In Bethlehem the holy;
Mary was the mother's name,
    Who lay in manger lowly.

Refrain—Sing, happy Virgin, mother mild;
    Sing, Joseph, father blessèd;
Sing, angels, shepherds, men so wise,
    For this thy Lord confessèd.

And as she in the manger lay,
    Beside the stallèd cattle,
A throng of shepherds entered in
    To hear the childish prattle.

The shepherds low obeisance made,
    Before the manger kneeling,
As thro' the casement's open space
    The star's bright ray came stealing.

The wingèd angel choir stood by,
    Their carol sweet a-singing;
While men of wisdom from the East,
    Drew near, their offerings bringing.

Then from the clouds was heard a voice,
    This message earthward sending,
" Peace rest upon the earth so fair,
    Good-will 'twixt men ne'er ending."

Although the lines seemed to go very well, I had great difficulty in hitting upon a suitable tune; but when once I did fit the verses to a composition of my

---

* Perhaps one of my musical readers will have the great kindness to set this little Carol to music, and let me see what it goes like to a tune that is musical and carol-like.

own, I howled it from morning till night all over the island. The very animals and birds must have been satiated with it. Possibly they would gladly have exchanged Christmas for Easter, or some other church festival, just for the sake of variety and change of tune.

One misty morning at the end of February, I was standing near the old cannon, chopping firewood wherewith to heat my oven, for it was my weekly baking day, when I saw a boat containing two men coming through the Creviçhon channel towards the house. One was pulling, and the other, who sat in the stern sheets, waved a white flag or handkerchief upon a stick, to attract my attention. I noticed them as soon as they did me, and waved in return, making signs for them not to land.

With my chopping hook still in my hand I ran down the rocky path towards them, and arrived at the water's edge just as they were about to run the boat ashore. I did not know what their intention in landing might be, so shook the chopper at them to warn them off. My stature, and the sight of my bare right arm, had their due effect, for they sheered off, a few boats' lengths, much to my relief. I soon found, however, that they were two of the men of Herm on a very peaceful mission, as they simply came to deliver a letter to me which a boat had brought over from St. Peter Port. I dare not speak, or could have asked them their mission, and they seemed quite dumbfounded at my bellicose attitude towards them.

The man in the stern now held up the letter, upon which I pantomimically intimated my wish that he should come close in and throw the letter to me. I then, lest they should be afraid to approach, threw my chopper as far behind me as I could, sending it clattering among the boulders nearly up to the cliff. Then the man in the stern folded the letter in two, and tied a piece of spun yarn round it, to which he attached a piece of stone, and tossed it to me. It fell fluttering near me, and I was almost afraid to pick it up, for fear it might contain some bad news of my family; but stooping, I secured it, placing it in my shirt bosom. Then by signs I expressed my thanks to the kind Hermese who had brought the missive.

When they had pulled out of sight towards Herm I sat down on a rock, and very mistrustfully drew forth the crumpled envelope. Was my father dead? What of Priscilla? Was mother ailing? These and a hundred other questions flashed across my mind as I slowly broke open the envelope. It was a letter from my dear old dad. Short, but quite assuring it ran:

"MY DEAR BOY,

"All is well. On the 2nd of March you will have occupied Jethou just twelve months. Some of my Yarmouth friends say I am cruel to allow you to stay alone so long, and think you must be so broken down by your exile, that nothing would keep you in Jethou six months longer. Young Johnson has even gone so far as to say he would wager you one hundred pounds you dare not stay another six months, and I therefore write to make known his offer, which I have in black and white, duly signed by him.

"Write me the word, YES or NO, *only*.

"Your affectionate Father,

"WILLIAM K. NILFORD."

What a curious letter from my father after all these months! Not a word as to himself, mother, or Priscilla. Not a line of news except the first three words, "All is well." That was assuring, at any rate, and made me feel happy. Young Johnson was the squire's son, a dashing, go-ahead fellow, but not greatly liked in the village, by reason of his haughtiness.

Although I had been looking forward to my return home I would not go to be laughed at by our Yarmouth friends; no, I would stay at all risks, and with the one hundred pounds I could make my future bride, Priscilla, a grand present. Yes, my mind was made up at once, and if the men had been within hail they might have come back and received my answer to send over to the St. Peter Port post office, from which the packet would take it to England, so that in about three or four days my father would receive it.

My answer was quickly written, for my reply was very laconic:

"*February 28th*, 18—.

"My Dear Father,

"All is well. I accept Johnson's wager of one hundred pounds, that I do not occupy Jethou for another six months.

"Your affectionate Son,

"HARRY NILFORD."

About noon I espied two men fishing off the nearest point of Herm, and going to the north-east corner of my island, to the promontory guarding Lobster Bay,

I signalled them with a handkerchief upon an ash sapling. They soon saw the signal and pulled towards me. As they neared me I was pleased to find they were the same two men who brought my father's letter to me in the morning. They came close into the bay, so that I had only to lean down and drop the letter into the boat, pointing towards St. Peter Port to signify I wanted it to go there by the first boat going.

"Oui, très bien."

Then I dropped half a crown (three francs) into their boat, and away they pulled, quite pleased. I went about my work, but in about twenty minutes, looking towards Guernsey, I saw the two men pulling away to St. Peter Port with my letter. This was more than I expected, as it would give them a rough pull of six miles. I only meant them to take the letter to Herm; but away it went, and a day was saved.

Away to my digging. I returned and forgot all about the men and the letter, but to my astonishment about four hours after, they hailed me, shouting and gesticulating, "C'est juste," they cried, and then away they went home, and I saw them no more.

CHAPTER XIII.

ANOTHER TERRIBLE STORM—LOSS OF THE "YELLOW BOY"—A KETCH WRECKED—I RESCUE A MAN FROM THE SEA, BADLY INJURED — HE RECOVERS.

FEBRUARY went out angrily, a heavy sea and a high wind being constant companions, but if February was wild the opening days of March were worse; it blew great guns and was cold also, and was decidedly unpleasant.

Beside the weather being unpleasant it was also a source of anxiety to me, for I had drawn the "Yellow Boy" upon a ledge of the Fauconnaire, above high water-mark; but now that the sea was in such a terrible rage, I was afraid it should dash over the ledge and dislodge her. If it did, nothing could save her. I could go over to her at low water, but could not draw her up higher, as the great rocks shelved out over her to the height of forty or fifty feet, and I had no tackling strong enough to raise her bodily to that awkward altitude; so I hoped and hoped on, but on the 4th of March matters came to a climax.

The sun rose red and angry, the wind blew in great

L

jerks and booms that staggered me as I walked along the perilously narrow paths. Just before high tide I walked along the lower path which, although fifty feet above the sea, was soaked with salt spray from the roaring coamers breaking below. The wind was so laden with spray that it was difficult to face it while staggering along the rugged cliff path; but presently I arrived at the point opposite the "Yellow Boy," and was glad to see her still there, although she was sadly buffeted by the waves, which continually leapt up to lick her off her granite cradle.

I had secured her with ropes as well as I could, and had even taken an anchor (attached to her mooring rope) some fifty feet up on a grassy ledge above, and there securely fixed it into the short turf, with which the first plateau of rocks were covered.

I sat down in my oilskins in the shelter of a rock to watch my precious boat, but I could see that her doom was sealed if the wind did not drop; but that it did not do, for as the tide rose, so did the wind, till it fairly howled among the rocks and tore through the trees in an awful rage, so that presently the ropes which bound the "Yellow Boy" gave way, as she was now very heavy, being level full of water. She only hung by the anchor rope now, like a man being hanged, and every wave that rose and broke in and around her, swung her from side to side, or spun her round till she gradually banged herself to pieces against the cruel granite walls. Then the tide gradually went down, and left the mere dangling skeleton of my once beloved craft, hanging high and dry above the send of the foaming waves, which at

"ALONG THE RUGGED CLIFF PATH."

intervals rushed among the now exposed rocks. The anchor held, and to the rope hung the two upper strakes, to which were attached the two fore compartments; all the rest was completely swept away, and with it my hope of again being able to take the sea for fishing, shooting, or sailing purposes. Alas! poor "Yellow Boy," I shall never see your like again! (neither probably will anyone else!) She answered my purpose admirably, but as a model of naval construction she was an absolute monstrosity, and would have made an object of great interest in a naval exhibition. I deeply regretted her loss, as I wanted to take her home as a great curiosity to open the eyes of the Yarmouth fishermen; but it was not to be, and I turned sadly away; my chief occupation (that of boating) being completely gone.

As I stood once more on the Cotills I saw two small vessels making for the Little Russel, or "Petit Ruan," as the Channel between Guernsey and Herm is called. They were labouring heavily, with very little canvas set, and evidently trying to gain the shelter of the islands, and if possible make for St. Peter's or St. Sampson's Harbour. Along they came, struggling and creeping closer, fathom by fathom, till just as the foremost was passing La Fauconnaire, her foremast snapped short off by the deck. In a moment she broached too, driving gradually broadside on to Jethou. The other finding she could not run into port, ran off towards Jersey where she might get better shelter, if it were not altogether a case of leaping out of the frying-pan into the fire, as the Jersey rocks are quite as hard and sharp as ours. At any rate in half an hour she was lost to sight.

The one which was now so helplessly driving towards where I stood was a trim little trading ketch of some fifty tons burthen, and from my elevated position I could see everything that took place on her deck. I saw the men (there were three men and a boy) cast out two anchors which appeared to hold her, then they commenced to cut away the mast and gear, which had fallen overboard and was thumping her sides so continuously as to cause grave apprehension of her being stove in. Having done this they rigged the pump, and at it they went with vigour. All their activity was required, as every wave that broke over her must have penetrated her seams, which were doubtless opened by the buffeting she had received. But alas! their noble efforts were all in vain, for with a snap, snap, which I could distinctly hear, her cables both broke, and she drifted quickly towards the shore. Seeing this, and thinking I might possibly be of some service, I ran down to a little wooden shelter I had built at the side of the Cotills, and procured a coil of thin rope, and slinging it over my shoulder I hurried back with it to the scene of what would probably be in a few minutes, a wreck.

When I got back, having only been absent three or four minutes, I saw that the crew had given up all hope of saving their vessel, and were now only intent on saving their lives. To this end they were getting their only boat out, lowering it safely on the lee side with two of the men and the boy in it; the third man, who appeared to be the skipper, would not leave the vessel, so the boat pushed off, but had not moved ten fathoms away when a tremendous sea curled up under its stern, and turned the boat a complete somersault, shooting the three occupants out into the water. They could none of them swim apparently, and in a few seconds disappeared beneath the turbulent waves; at least I did not see them again, so that doubtless they found a watery grave.

The last man evidently saw his danger, but was quite calm, although his end seemed near, as only about two hundred yards now intervened between the vessel and the rocky shore. He proceeded to lash a spar across the two water barrels, which he emptied and bunged up, and then stood ready to jump overboard with them, when the vessel struck. I also was on the alert with my coil of rope, following the vessel as she drifted slowly along the shore, till she neared a spur of cliff, which runs out near the watch-house, close to the homestead, and here she came in full contact with a mass of rock which shook her, crushed in her stem, and made her recoil. The next wave threw her back again, but luckily more steadily, so that I was enabled to throw my coil of rope down upon her deck from my coign of vantage. I quickly whipped the shore end round the stem of a huge furze bush, which grew within ten feet of the brink of the cliff, and to my joy found that the man had seized the end which I had thrown towards him. He stood amidship, being afraid to venture too close to the bows, as the next wave would doubtless ram the ship hard against the rocks again, and if he jumped now, he would simply be smashed to pieces between the rocks and the vessel.

He waited, holding on to the coamings of the

hatchway, which had been burst open, till the little ketch gave another tremendous leap upon the cruel rocks, and then as she recoiled he sprang to his feet, threw over his barrel life preserver, and without hesitation leaped overboard with the rope round his chest just beneath his arms. He swam, and I hauled, and as he mounted the next wave I slackened, or he might have been dashed to pieces, then on the wave breaking and running back, I hauled with all my might, and in a short time had him safe in my arms, and bore him amid the dashing spray and foam safely beyond danger. He was just able to stand, and that was all, for directly I had half dragged and half carried him up the cliffs to a grassy spot, he fell backwards insensible. He could not have been in the sea more than two minutes, yet he was terribly cut about, his hands being covered with blood; some of his fingers were cut to the bone. This was done when the first wave threw him against the rocks, when all depended upon his being able to hold on against the receding water. He did in his despair hold on, as he afterwards described it, "like a limpet," and thus though terribly battered he was saved, the sole survivor of his little crew.

When he came to, I assisted him up to the house, where I gave him some hot grog and more solid refreshment, and then prepared him a warm bath. Poor fellow! his legs made me shudder to look at them, so cruelly had the rocks torn and lacerated them from the knee downward. Yet in his terrible state the brave fellow was quite beside himself with joy at his miraculous escape, while the next minute the hot tears would gush from his eyes at the thought of his poor messmates, who had sailed their last voyage, and were now floating about to be devoured by the huge congers, crabs, and lobsters, which are so numerous in these deep seas.

A long night's rest greatly restored my guest, who had come to me *à la* Friday in "Robinson Crusoe;" in fact, I felt an almost irresistible longing to call him Friday, and introduce myself to him as R. Crusoe, Esq.; but when I looked at his pale face and hands swathed in huge bandages, I concluded it to be an ill time for any joking. After a day or two's rest and unceasing attention to his wounds on my part, I was pleased to find him greatly improved both in body and spirits, and therefore felt that I might ask him a little about himself. What information he gave me I will here epitomise.

He was by name Alexander Ducas, a son of France, his native village being situate on the Bay of Avranches, facing Jersey. He was about my own age, but had seen more ups and downs than most men of double his years. He had been in the French navy; had been mate of several vessels; had also taken charge of several English yachts; had been skipper of two or three small trading vessels, and finally had become owner and skipper of the little ketch which had met with such a disastrous end a few days before. This was not the first nor the second time he had narrowly escaped death by drowning; but as he afterwards told me, "he thought he had done with the *surface* of the water," and probably had I not opportunely been on the spot, he

RESCUE OF ALEC DUCAS.

would have shared the fate of his poor crew, none of whose bodies were ever seen again.

"Why did you throw overboard your water barrel life preserver; before you clutched my rope," I asked him.

"A double chance," he replied, "for if the rope business had failed, I might still have secured the aid of the barrels to support me. A poor chance I allow, but a *chance* nevertheless."

He was of medium height, fair, with sandy moustache, compactly knit, and of surprising strength for a man of his inches. I afterwards found that he was possessed with more than an ordinary amount of physical endurance, for no matter how much work he crowded into a long summer's day, he was always as blithe as a cricket when work was over, and we sat by the old cannon to smoke an evening pipe and chat together about our plans and prospects.

Strange to say, he knew the man I buried at sea some months before, in fact, had sailed with him on one vessel for several months, and he moreover gave him a very bad character. It appears that he was a most desperate fellow, having been in prison on several occasions for violent conduct, and was noted for his brutal language and bad behaviour. He had been turned out of the French navy for insubordination, and while on the frigate was a perfect terror to his messmates. He was noted as the strongest man of the three hundred who formed her crew, and as Ducas said, "There won't be enough tears shed over his death by the friends who knew him to wet a postage stamp!"

What a lucky thing for me this man did not become *my* comrade.

By the end of a week Ducas, or as I more familiarly called him Alec, was able to take short walks, and the more he saw of the island the better he liked it, and finally asked to be allowed to stay with me, and cultivate the land, and render what service he could in other ways.

I was in a quandary to know how to answer him, as I did not know how it would affect my agreement with Young Johnson "to stay on the island for six months longer." I therefore told Alec I would let him know my decision in four days from then, giving myself that time to turn the matter over in my mind.

So far as the agreement with my father went that was concluded, as my twelve months had already expired; but what I was puzzled about was how I should stand with Johnson. It seemed to me that he expected me to remain *alone* on the island for the specified time—six months—but what was I to do now man Friday had arrived? I puzzled over the matter a long time, and then came to the conclusion that win or lose I would stay on the island another summer, and whether I transgressed the contract or not, I would retain Ducas, as it would be very pleasant to have a companion, and if I was by so doing breaking the contract, must abide by the consequences.

I next interviewed Alec Ducas, and found that between his sea engagements he had assisted in gardening and the usual routine of farm work, beside which, being a thorough seaman, he could make his own clothes and boots, consequently mine; in fact, could turn his hand to anything, as only a sailor can.

"Well, Ducas, I am going to stay here for another six months; you have seen the resources of the house and island, and can judge best, if you think you would rather stay here than go over to St. Peter Port in prospect of getting another vessel. What do you say, would you rather go or stay?"

To this he made reply, his face beaming with delight,

"Well, sir, I have not much of a mind to make up, but if you will allow me to stay and help you, nothing will give me greater pleasure; in fact, such a life is the one I crave. There is liberty for a man here, and plenty of work to be done, and I have ample health and strength to do it, so if you will say 'Yes,' I will take up my quarters with you."

He spoke very good English, but with a decidedly foreign accent (which sounded very pleasant to me, more so as he had a very musical voice), and was a plain spoken man, one who called a spade a spade, and made no nonsense about it.

"Very well, Alec," said I; "then you stay, and I trust we may get along happily together."

CHAPTER XIV.

WORK AND SONG — SUNDAY SERVICE — BUILD A LARGER BOAT, THE "ANGLO-FRANC"— COLLECTING WRECKAGE — COMMENCE A JETTY — OUR COOKERY — BLASTING OPERATIONS — THE OPENING BANQUET.

DURING the remainder of March we worked away merrily in the garden and in the fields on the top of the island. I was really astonished at the work we could get through in a day, Alec, myself, and the donkey. Alec laughed at my plough and the cart, and together we made some improvements in them. We also improved the lower path right round the island, by cutting away the furze and undergrowth; with spade and pick we made it broader in the narrowest parts, and by filling the inequalities, made it comfortable to walk upon.

Alec was a wonder for singing; in fact he was warbling all day long over his work, and I must say he had rather a nice tenor voice, just such as an Englishman would expect a Frenchman to possess. His répertoire of songs was large, and embraced both ancient and modern, sacred and secular, French and English; so there was plenty of variety.

Somehow or other, although he was of a most lively disposition, most of his "best songs," as he called those he could sing with the greatest ease and effect, were of the somewhat dismal or semi-lachrymose type, as "Tom Bowling," "Half Mast High," "The Skipper and his Boy," etc. These are all beautiful in their way, but with repetition pall upon one somewhat, while your jovial song seems ever fresh, and will stand singing many times before it becomes threadbare.

Sometimes of an evening, after supper and a pipe, we would indulge in duet singing, and when we came to the end of the song we would praise each other and encore ourselves.

"Let's have that one again. That's capital! Bravo!"

Then at it we would go again, sometimes till near midnight.

I had an old volume of sea songs in my trunk, several of which we both knew, as "All's Well," "Larboard Watch," "The Anchor's Weighed," etc. Alec's tenor and my deep baritone harmonized rather well, so we thoroughly enjoyed ourselves. As we had no hearers we used to give wonderful expression to our singing, possibly it was lucky no one could hear us, for it would certainly unstring their nerves.

On Sundays we did no work, but at eleven o'clock had a kind of service which lasted quite an hour and a half. I was parson and read the service, while Alec was clerk and read the lessons and made the responses, while, to pass the time away, we always sang two hymns wherever only one should be sung. This was to give each of us an opportunity of selecting his favourites. There was no levity in all this, we did it as a duty to our Maker, in thankfulness for the manifold blessings bestowed upon us during the week; for our health, welfare, and all the other blessings which He bestowed upon us from day to day. Alec had great cause to be thankful that he had been spared ever to put foot on land again, while I, beside my numerous lucky escapes, had not had a day's real illness since I landed. Before I left the island, Sankey and Moody's "Sacred Songs" would scarcely hold together, so much had it suffered from being turned by our great rough thumbs and fingers, while to say that some of the pages were slightly soiled was putting it in a very mild manner. A stranger might have thought that we hid the volume up the chimney, when not in use, and the appearance would quite have warranted his surmise.

Our first great work together was to build another boat, a larger one than the "Yellow Boy," and on an improved principle. First we collected whatever we thought would be of use in the construction of our craft, which we christened, before a stick of her was laid, "The Anglo-Franc." This was a curious commencement, I must own, but then we did some very strange things on Jethou. The name was chosen because we, as shipwrights, were respectively English and French. We scoured the whole island for material, and succeeded in getting a huge pile together from various sources, thus we were not so cramped as when I built the famous "Yellow Boy."

Speaking of the "Yellow Boy" reminds me that

after the big storm I saved the portion which still depended from the cable, suspended from the side of La Fauconnaire. These pieces were the two upper strakes, fifteen feet long, and the fore and second compartments. The timber from these helped us greatly in the building of the new boat. Besides this there were a number of rafters and floor boards that I had collected from the old store-house after the explosion; but our third and best supply was obtained from the wreck of Alec's ketch, "Jeanette," the fore part of which still remained jammed high up between two rocks, which stood about twelve feet apart, near high-water mark, on La Creviçhon. From this, by dint of three days' hard work, we secured several loads of deck-timber and other very useful pieces, which "Eddy" dragged up for us to the ruined store-house.

We found our cart wheels were not high enough to clear the big stones on the beach, so we took them off and replaced them by two runners so as to form a kind of sledge, which answered much better, although many pieces were jerked off *en route*, by reason of the rugged path and primitive construction of the sledge. As Alec remarked, they served as guide posts, so that there was no losing the way. This idea I got by reading Catlin's "North American Indians." By lashing two long tent poles at a horse's sides, with the ends trailing on the ground, they form a kind of sledge, upon which they can carry considerable loads upon transverse sticks.

From the battered hulk we also brought a great number of bolts and other iron-work, a companion ladder, windlass, pump, bowsprit bits, bell, a torn jib, a quantity of cordage, and whatever else we could lay our hands upon, that might have the most remote chance of being of future use to us.

In story books it is usual to have a ship come ashore just in a convenient spot, and with a full cargo; but ours, unfortunately, was only half a battered hulk, perfectly empty, and in a most awkward position to get at, as we had to cross the Creviçhon Channel at every trip, so that we could only bring the wreckage over at low tide. We could, however, continue our work of dismantling right through the day, except for two hours, when the high tide flowed in and out through poor "Jeanette's" ribs. These two hours we took for rest, food, and the soothing pipe. Bless Raleigh!

When we had collected all our material, both iron and wood, we commenced building the "Anglo-Franc," and in three weeks had her finished and afloat. She was sixteen feet over all, by five feet beam, and was rigged in the style peculiar to the Guernsey boats; that is to say she had two small masts. The foremast was stepped exactly amidships, while the mizen was placed close to the stern. This arrangement strikes an Englishman as very strange, as they are in the habit of seeing the foremast very nearly in the bows; but Ducas was a sailor, and knew the rig adapted to these waters, and I must say that under most circumstances the "Anglo-Franc" behaved herself admirably. She was a success in every way. One special feature was, that we built a kind of half-deck forward, which formed a small cuddy or cabin quite large enough for one of us to have "a watch below" in, or for a regular sleep at night, or we could both squeeze inside during a pelting rain. We spent several single nights at sea in the "Anglo-Franc" during the summer, and by putting a sail-cloth awning from the aft edge of the cuddy deck we lengthened our cabin by four feet, and could thus both obtain a good night's rest, or cook in any wind or weather.

When we had finished the boat we were rather at a loss to know how to find accommodation for her when we did not actually require to use her. In fine weather she could lie moored just off the house, and to enable us always to keep her afloat, we rigged up an out-haul, so that standing on the shore we could haul the boat out or in to its moorings whenever we chose. This was all very well in fine weather, but when a fresh south-west wind was blowing, and a heavy sea on, she would pitch and roll to such an extent that we were afraid she would break loose and drift away. We had therefore to cast about for some safer place for her, and with this in view inspected the whole island round. When we came to Lobster Bay, at the north-east corner, we agreed that that was the most sheltered position we could find, and most suitable in every way for a haven.

Quite at the angle of the island a promontory runs straight out to the eastward for a distance of about forty yards, thus forming a shelter from the rush of the rising tide through the Perchée Channel, while the island of Herm kept the wind from the north-east in check.

"Now," said Alec, "if we could build a little stone breakwater from the end of Cape Homard (Cape

Lobster, as Alec called the point, because we kept the lobster and crab pots there), we could make as safe a little harbour as one could wish for."

This proposition seemed all very well, but the quantity of stone I knew it would take rather staggered me, and I was a long time before I could be brought to give my consent to help in the matter. But when Alec had laid out his plans to me, I found them so consistent that I readily agreed to help in the work.

Without wearying the reader by describing in too great detail the building of our breakwater, I will just give an outline of how it was built, and another great success achieved, although to ensure that success we had to work like a couple of galley slaves. Still, with all our hard work, we were as happy as a couple of schoolboys. We toiled, sang, and ate with such appetites as only those who are used to hard work in the sea air can know.

Our plan was to work on Monday; enjoy fishing, etc., on Tuesday; work on Wednesday at the breakwater, at the garden on Thursday; on Friday at the breakwater again; and on Saturday till noon also, after which we devoted the rest of the day to baking, clothes washing and mending, and other domestic duties. How my mother and 'Cilla would have laughed to see me at the wash-tub, or hanging out the linen to dry on the furze bushes; or to have seen Alec using a flat iron which, with great labour, we had forged, and which was of a peculiar construction, but still very efficacious in its work. Men are notoriously awkward in their manner of wringing and other laundry work, and I expect we were no exception to the general rule. We made our clothes *clean*, and that was all we required.

Alec was a capital baker, so we had some excellent bread, while my pastry was not to be sneezed at; in fact, at a rabbit pie I was quite a *grand chef*. I also introduced several new culinary matters to Alec, some of which he had never seen before; among them being the all-filling Norfolk dumpling, which at first he did not seem to care for, but in time he became inordinately fond of them, and would often ask me to make him a *pouding de rien* (a pudding of nothing), which was his idea of these articles of everyday diet in East Anglia.

But I am not building my breakwater of dumplings, so will get back to stone; not that I wish the reader to infer that my dumplings were ever approaching that substance in their degree of firmness.

First we collected all the very large stones we could find in the bay, and placed them as a foundation for our breakwater; but these only formed a layer about a foot deep. All these were large stones (some of them weighed nearly three hundredweight), so to cope with them we made a kind of four-handled hand barrow, upon which we rolled our rock, and then taking two handles each, staggered off with it. These large pieces we placed near the end of the breakwater, and when we had denuded the bay, we obtained, with " Eddy's " help, some large piece of massed rock and mortar from the ruined boathouse. These pieces we took in the sledge, and built into a kind of wall to form the outer shell of the breakwater, while the interior we filled with any odds and ends of rocks (none of them less than a man's head in size) which we could find on the shore. The interstices we filled with shingle, and the detritus of granite, but when we had raised our structure to the level of high water our available stone gave out. This rather non-plussed us, but at last we decided to open a small quarry and see what granite we could obtain to raise our undertaking another four feet in height.

I had still several pounds of gunpowder left, and with part of this we constructed some long thin cartridges for blasting. With these, a pick-axe, and some long iron stanchions, which we used as levers, we obtained a good supply of stone. The little quarry may still be seen, so I am informed, although it is greatly covered with furze and weeds. It is situated on the hill side, midway between the homestead and the ruins of the boathouse. We chose an elevated position for our quarry, so that we could roll the huge stones down the hill to the pathway below, where we levered them up into the sledge, and dragged them to what we were pleased to term "the works." Let it suffice to say that about the middle of May our task was completed, and to commemorate the event we gave a grand banquet on the pier head (for we called it a pier now, as it sounded more dignified) to commemorate the event. Four of us sat down to the banquet, or rather two stood and two sat. As architect I took the head of the table (a wine cask), and Alec, as engineer, the foot; while "Eddy," the donkey, as contractor, supported me on the right (dining luxuriously on a bunch of carrots and some hay), and on my left was dear old "Begum" as clerk of the works, enjoying two whole rabbits as his share of the entertainment.

We drank "Success to Jethou Pier," and trusted it would take every care of the "Anglo-Franc," which we now placed within its encircling arm for the first time.

At low water we removed all the big stones from the little haven in which our boat was now moored. This was for fear she might hurt her bottom (as the tide left her careened half an hour before dead low water), and thus made everything snug for her. At half-tide she floated, so that for six hours out of every twelve we could go off just when we liked, without any pushing or hard work of any kind; while to assist her to her moorings, if we wished to bring her in at low tide, we rigged up the windlass which we brought from the wreck, and thus we could at any time haul her bodily out of the sea.

Now, having given up a whole chapter to hard work, we will proceed to something a little more interesting and exciting.

CHAPTER XV.

TRAWLING FOR FISH AND DREDGING FOR CURIOS—SOME REMARKABLE FINDS—A GHASTLY RESURRECTION — THE MYSTERIOUS PAPER — THE HIEROGLYPHIC—A DANGEROUS FALL—HORS DE COMBAT—ATTEMPTS TO UNRAVEL THE PAPER.

AS there were now two of us we occasionally had a turn at trawling, and usually caught some fine flat fish, turbot, soles, and plaice. Our net was a very primitive one of our own manufacture, and had to be handled very gingerly, as the netting was old and the ironwork very fragile, but knowing this we did not put undue strain upon it.

The curious fish, marine plants, and odds and ends of all kinds that we brought to the surface would have done a naturalist's heart good, for there were frequently objects brought to light that were quite out of the common.

It seemed to me that the set of the Gulf Stream had something to do with this, as we found some rare shells that did not appear indigenous to these waters; we also found two old swords and the steel portion of a flint lock pistol, beside some curious old pottery, all of which finds I have preserved, and with other curios have formed quite a museum.

Our plan of "Marine Exploration," as we called it, was this: We would have a couple of hours trawling for fish in the usual manner, and then if wind and tide were favourable, would run in and land our trawl, and fish at the pier head, and bring out with us another implement, which was a cross between a dredge and a trawl. It had an iron beam about six feet wide, which kept the net on the bottom by reason of its weight; from this rose an iron bow, forming a flattened half circle, and to this was attached a piece of heavy double netting, the bottom of which was protected from the rocks by a piece of old sail cloth a little larger than the plan of the net. The poke of the net was only about seven feet from beam to tail, so that we had no difficulty in raising it, especially as we had a line fastened to the tail, which one of us could haul upon, while the other (with a curious hand windlass, which looked like some diabolical instrument of torture) raised the beam.

We used to drain the net fairly well before bringing it inboard, and then turn the contents out on the floor, then kneeling down we would search among them just like a couple of misers counting their gold; indeed, upon one occasion, we *did* have gold to count among our other items.

It was the bowl portion of a golden goblet, from which the foot had become detached. From its encrusted appearance it must have lain for many years in the sea. On another occasion we felt something heavy in the net as we hauled, and knowing that in the spot in which we were then trawling, there were no rocks, we naturally wondered what it could be. As we hove up the net, I remarked that I hoped it was not a dead body, which remark made Alec feel quite queer, as he thought it might be one of his comrades. He refused to help me haul for fear such should be the case. I quickly pointed out to him that it could not be the case, as apart from a corpse being devoured by the voracious fish, it would swell as it decomposed, and gas being formed in it, it would buoy the body up, and float it to the surface, when the send of the waves would waft it away, no one knew whither.

"Now," said I to Alec, "your messmates have been dead these four months, and nothing of them now remains round this island, except perchance their skeletons, and we are not likely to come upon *them*, so bear a hand and let's see what luck has sent us."

Slowly the net came up, and as the water left it there appeared among the brown seaweed two huge pieces of rock tied to something which looked very horrid. And horrid it turned out to be, for it was the remains of the man I had buried months before, that is to say, the leg bones, with some few remaining tendons and other parts, which the fish had not stripped from the bones. We were glad to find that the upper part with the skull attached had fallen off, so turning the net inside out, I for a second time buried the poor man, or rather all that was left of him.

One day in July, a very warm day, we had been

fishing and caught but little, so were having an hour's chat and smoke as our boat rocked lazily on the clear blue water, when somehow the conversation turned on curious discoveries and accidental finds. Suddenly the thought of my valuable discovery of the lace entered my head. Should I tell Alec? No! I would keep my secret; but what of the paper I had discovered in the niche in the wall? Could not Alec decipher that for me? Should I tell him of that? Why not? By keeping the paper to myself I should not know if it were of value or no, so revolving the matter in my mind as to how I should broach the subject, I at last made up my mind to consult him upon the subject, but said nothing of it just then. We set to work again, after a rest, and fished, but fortune that day was not kind to us, or the fish were as lazy as ourselves; anyhow, we caught very few; in fact, not more than we could consume in a fresh state. When we obtained plenty we gutted them, split them, took off their heads, and dried them in the sun for future use, just as the natives of the Pacific Islands do theirs.

That evening, when supper was finished, I told Alec I had something to shew him, which did not belong to me, but which might or might not be of value to me as the holder.

Somehow I had, by associating the old leathern cup and the lace together, brought myself to believe that the paper was like the lace, of some value. Therefore it behoved me to be careful as to how I broached the subject to Alec.

I quietly took it from my trunk, and handed it to him carelessly, with the remark,

"Can you read that for me, Alec?"

He had a good look at it, holding it very close to the lamp, and read it quite through to himself, while I sat impatiently waiting for him to say something about it. Not wishing to appear anxious I pretended to read, but although I looked at the page it might just as well have been a brick I was looking at as a book for all the information I got from it.

At length he laid the paper down, and informed me that he could read it well enough, but what did it all refer to?

"It is a list of articles followed by some curious signs that I cannot make out," said he. "Then it goes on to say that anyone finding the things mentioned, may have them as a gift for his trouble in searching for them. Then follows the date, Nov. 13, 17—. So probably your musty old paper is at least one hundred years old."

Then he laid the document on the table, relit his pipe, and went on cutting out a netting needle for to-morrow's use. I merely remarked it was an old paper I had had by me a long time, and as I wanted to know what it was about had kept it. With that I put it away in the trunk, and changed the subject by turning my attention to snooding a score or two of fish hooks for conger fishing.

Next day when I saw an opportunity I got away to a quiet spot, and puzzled myself with the hieroglyphic-looking portion of the paper which appeared thus:—

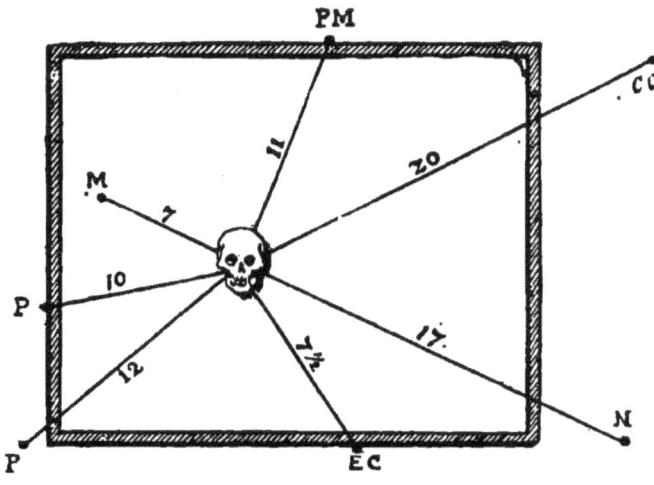

—THE PUZZLING DOCUMENT—

I puzzled over it for an hour, and then gave it up, not having obtained the slightest clue to the meaning, if any meaning it had. Then I reflected that a man was not likely to go to the trouble of writing out a long list of articles, and sketching a skull with particular lines and figures radiating from it for nought, to say nothing of hiding the paper away in such a cosy little nook as the one in which I found it. Thus reflecting I turned along the middle path homeward, wondering if some old privateer skipper, or even pirate, had long years ago hidden the articles mentioned in the list in some part of the island, or could it refer to some treasure which—*slip! bump! crash!!*

* * * * *

I opened my eyes and found Alec bending over me, while "Begum" sat licking my hand. I tried to speak, but did so with extreme difficulty, as if something were amiss with my chest. Whatever had happened! I tried to rise, but had not the power.

"How do you feel?" said Alec.

A TERRIBLE FALL FROM THE CLIFFS.

To which I replied by asking him a question, "Whatever is the matter, Alec, am I hurt?" at which he laughed and said, "I ought to know better than he could tell me; perhaps I would inform him what I was doing there, and why, for more than half an hour since he found me I had been insensible?"

Then I remembered slipping carelessly over the edge of the path at a part that was not at all dangerous, and bumping myself against a granite rock, but beyond that I remembered nothing whatever.

Alec had missed me for nearly three hours, so calling to "Begum," he strolled along to see what I was doing. It was our invariable custom to tell each other where we were going, and what we were going to do, whenever we separated for a time; but on this occasion I had purposely omitted this precaution. The dog had found me on the lower pathway doubled up, or as Alec put it, "Standing on my head in a very undignified position, with my back against a granite boulder."

I could not rise, in fact could scarcely move, so battered and bruised was I in my fall of about fifty yards. Of course this was not a perpendicular fall, or I should never have penned these lines; but as the slope was one that a man could not walk up without using his hands, it is a wonder to me to this day that I was not killed on the spot. Evidently I had broken my swift fall by clutching at some furze bushes, for my right hand was dreadfully lacerated, and full of furze needles, and my shoulder so stiff that my arm seemed paralyzed; besides which, I found I was spitting blood, which frightened me very much, as I was afraid of some internal injury.

The cart was fetched, and Alec assisted me on it; but oh dear me! I thought the jolting would have shaken me literally to pieces, so I sang out "Halt! Wo!" and told Alec I could go no farther, and then I fainted away.

It was only of five minutes' duration, but when I

came to I felt as if I was dying, and told Alec I thought my time had come, which greatly alarmed the good fellow.

"Do you mind my leaving you a few minutes," said he, "while I fire the big gun for assistance?"

"No, no, Alec, I will not consent to that ; for if my time has come, all the doctors* in the world cannot save me; and if I am not so badly hurt as I fear, I shall pull through. Assist me to get on 'Eddy's' back."

By great exertion on the part of Alec, and great forbearance from crying out on mine, I was presently mounted on the donkey, and being supported on Alec's broad shoulder as he walked on the left side, I was at length able to reach the house.

Although in dreadful pain, I could not resist asking Alec if he did not notice how well our group on the rocky path realized the parable of the Good Samaritan. Here we were carrying out the story

---

* Speaking of island doctors reminds me that Dr. Moyle has recently retired from practice in the Isles of Scilly, where he has been the sole medical practitioner for over forty years. He is spoken of with love and respect by all the islanders, and no wonder, for he has been a wonderful old man. His patients were scattered over the five inhabited islands, and never once did he fail to go when summoned. On many a wild winter night has he been called up to cross the rough sea to attend, perhaps, on some poor fisherman's child. Dressed in an oilskin coat, sou' wester and big boots, he was always ready to go, and scarcely looked like a medical man. The people have shown their regard for him in a handsome manner. Without the aid of bazaars or other such institutions, they have raised funds enough to present him with a life-long annuity of £52.

exactly. I was the "Certain Man" wounded; Alec the Good Samaritan; and "Eddy" the beast.

The house being reached, next came the dreadful dismounting, and being supported to bed; but even this was at last safely managed, and lying on the coverlet for a time I felt much easier.

Alec busied himself like a trained nurse, he took off my boots, gave me some brandy, washed the blood from my head and hands, and then without my knowledge gave me a sleeping draught from my medicine chest.

When I awoke it was still daylight, and Alec had prepared me a good supper, with which, like a good fellow, he fed me, and then we held a consultation as to the nature of my hurts.

We tried each leg, but beyond great black bruises there were no bones broken; my hands were a mass of cuts and scratches, and my head was in no better condition; but when we came to the right arm we found something radically wrong at the shoulder, which had now become greatly swollen, while as I sat on the edge of the bed the limb hung loosely down in a way that caused us to think it was broken; at any rate it was perfectly useless.

We consulted Dr. Ogilvie's book upon all kinds of accidents that bones are heir to, and came to the conclusion that either my collar bone was broken or displaced, or my arm was out of the socket at the shoulder.

Alec soon set to work, and ripped my coat and shirt off, and after a deliberate diagnosis of my upper man, concluded that my shoulder was out of joint and must be put in. Again my comrade wished to fire the big gun for assistance, but I made up my mind to attempt my own cure with his help, as I had seen several cases of a similar nature treated on the hunting field.

My arm is a strong one, and I must draw a veil over the agony which resulted from the clumsy way in which we hauled the poor limb about; but we clicked the bone in at last, and then faint from pain I must have gone off into a deep sleep, for the last I remember was feeling Alec wipe the perspiration from my forehead as I fell back on my pillow in a faint.

For days I kept my bed, as every part of my anatomy had received a tremendous battering when I took my flight over the jagged stones that barred my way.

My constant thought as I lay on the bed with the glorious sunshine streaming in from the open window, which gave me a view of the dark trees standing out against the azure sunlit sky, was about the hieroglyphics on the paper. What did the skull portend, and what did the letters and figures refer to?

The skull I set down as the point to which the most importance was to be attached, and as I believed it referred to some hidden articles or treasure stowed away more than a century ago, I was naturally very eager to find out its whereabouts.

Well, say the skull represented the treasure spot, what did the square surrounding it mean? I gave it up. "Then what," I asked myself, "is the meaning of the letters at certain angles round the square both inside and out?" These I assumed to be the bearings of certain objects, as the person stood at the spot in which the goods were hidden; the figures I conjectured were the number of feet or yards distant of the "treasure spot" from the various objects.

Next, where was it most likely a man would hide anything of value, beneath the sea or upon dry land? Land certainly. Would it be among the rocks or where the ground was softer? Certainly the latter, I should say.

Then I set to thinking of the different places on the island where the nature of the soil would allow of digging, and could call to mind but few, and these mostly on the higher parts of the island. I determined when I was able to get about that I would inspect all these places, and see if I could find objects to correspond with the bearings and distances given in the sketch. Having thus promised myself to pursue the search further at a more appropriate time, I dismissed the subject from my mind for the time being.

After several days of enforced idleness I was at length able once more to go out, but at first felt very weak in the legs for want of exercise.

CHAPTER XVI.

YARNS: THE CABBAGES WHICH HUNG THEIR HEADS—THE RAFT OF SPRUCE—VOYAGE OF THE "DEWDROP"—A LUCKY FAMILY—A DEEP, DEEP DRAUGHT—THE MAIRE'S CAT.

ALEC behaved splendidly while I was unable to help myself. He fished, and by hook or by crook—or rather, by hook and by net—procured whatever I cared for, beside which he killed the surviving pig, which had now grown into an immense fellow, so that we had a good supply of meat, although somewhat fat; but of this I ate little, preferring a more vegetable diet, although at times I took a little meat, but not often. When the day's work was over he would sit in the twilight and spin yarns to me of his own curious experiences, one or two of which I cannot refrain from repeating here.

"Did you ever do any smuggling?" I asked him one day.

"Well," said he, "that's rather personal, is it not? But still, I may as well tell you truly—I have. But as it is now very risky work, and some of my experience is recent, I shall not tell you of my own adventures in that line of business, though I see but little harm in outwitting a revenue officer, and at the same time enabling your neighbours to obtain a luxury or two, which otherwise they would never have. Did I ever do any smuggling? Rather! and my father and grandfather before me. In fact, in the village of my birth a man is thought little of who has not, at some time or other, been 'smarter than a revenue officer.'"

These remarks aroused my curiosity, so I asked, "Were you ever caught at the game?"

"No," said he, "but I'll tell you how my father was once bowled over by the sun taking part against him. It was in the month of August, 185—, that he had, by manœuvring, brought ashore quite a nice little lot of contraband during the night, and not liking to keep it in the house, placed a couple of men on watch while he buried it in the garden. He had a little plot of cabbages near one side of the garden, and he uprooted about a dozen of these in the middle of the patch; then, digging a somewhat shallow hole, he placed his goods in, and re-casting the mould back, replanted the cabbages, not forgetting to remove the surplus mould in pails. So far so good; but early the next morning a customs officer had, by some means, heard that my father had been seen in his boat on the previous day, in close proximity to a trading vessel which had signalled for water, one of her casks having been started by the heat. Of course my father was very pleased to see the officer (or apparently so), and after showing him over the place, invited him to stay to breakfast, which he gladly did. About ten o'clock he took his departure, apparently quite as satisfied with his visit, as my father was pleased at his departure. All seemed very easy now—simply to wait till dark, when one or two friends would divide the haul and take it away in some secret manner. But a little after noon back came the officer, accompanied by another. Here was evidently something in the wind, and my father felt very anxious.

"'Very sorry to trouble you, M. Ducas, but duty is duty, you know. Will you kindly accompany us over your premises?'

"'Certainly.'

"Then they searched high and low, but nothing could they find. Dinner was being served. Would they join us at table?

"'Thanks, very pleased to.'

"So they sat down. My father, after dinner, handed them a bottle of the 'right sort,' of which they were connoisseurs, and they enjoyed it. It was a hot day, and everything was greatly in want of rain, and being so hot and dry they strolled out into the garden, preparatory to taking their leave.

"'How are monsieur's pigs? Oh, ah, very fine fellows! Do you give them much green food?'

"'Yes, a fair amount,' my father replied, and pulling up the nearest cabbage to him, threw it to the animals.

"'What a pity to waste such a fine cabbage,' said the chief officer. 'Why not give them one of those which are languishing so for want of water?' and reaching over he made a big pull at one, which, to his astonishment, came out of the ground without any resistance. 'Hello! what's this, Ducas? Why, all the middle ones seem to be in a sad way! See, they are hanging their heads. Perhaps the soil is not congenial to their growth. *Have you a spade?*'

"It was all up. The spade had to be forthcoming, and the end of it was,—' Fined two hundred francs or thirty-five days in prison.'"

"Well, Alec, that's not half bad. Spin us another."

"Ah, well, I could spin you enough yarns to make a frigate's cable, and a thick one too, if you would only listen to them."

"Very good. Then let me have another strand towards the said ship's cable; but don't spin it *too thick.*"

"Let's see, which one shall I give you? Oh, I know; but it's one that did *not* end in a fine, though it was a very close shave. I was quite a youngster, but anything but a green hand at the business, for I had accompanied my father on many occasions on which he did not bring home merely soles or *longuenez* for freight. Just before the occasion of which I am about to tell you there had been a gale, and during the worst of the blow a Norwegian vessel had jettisoned her deck load of spruce poles, and we being out fishing a day or two after, happened, as luck would have it, to fall in with some of them. As we had some spare rope aboard we made a kind of raft of them, and commenced towing them towards the harbour, which was only five or six miles distant.

"Now it so happened that a fishing boat passed us as we tugged our timber along, and what is more remarkable, upon my father holding up a white pail a man at the stern of the lugger did the same, then altering her canvas she made a tack (where one was not required), and coming very close to us dropped overboard a series of black tin cases, which were no doubt hermetically sealed, to preserve their contents. These cylinders were so nicely balanced that the rounded sides of them just showed above the water, and no more. Some more cabalistic signs then passed between my father and the lugger's skipper, as she stood away on her course, and in an hour was out of sight round the cape. We made fast the cylinders (which were attached to a rope) *underneath* the raft, and standing in for shore and entered the little port.

"We moored our logs, and my father at once went to the authorities and reported the finding of *a raft*, and as usual an officer came down to inspect and put a mark on the timbers. His inspection was finished, and he was about to go upon other business when a boy who had, with some companions, been scampering about the raft, fell into the water. At once a number of men jumped on the raft, which was nearly submerged by the additional weight; but what was worse the cordage binding the logs together gave way, and behold, bobbing among the floating men were seen a series of floating cylinders! The men were hauled out of the water, and so were the curious tin cases, while with the latter my father was hauled off to appear before the magistrates on a charge of smuggling."

"A clear case I should say, Alec," I remarked.

"Well, so everyone thought; but, strange to say, my father was discharged with a caution. The turning point of the case was, did we pick up separate logs of timber and construct the raft, or did we find the raft *already made?* Our case was that we had picked up the *whole* raft at sea, and not having examined it, were not supposed to know what was hanging beneath it. Beside which, had not M. Ducas gone straight away and given notice to the proper authorities? We obtained the benefit of the doubt, but it was a very close squeak."

"It was indeed. Now do you not remember any little adventure of your own you could tell me?"

"Adventures! I could fill a whole book with them; some of them so strange that they would appear to most people more like falsehoods than solid fact."

"But, you know, Alec, it is only a hair line that frequently separates the sublime from the ridiculous, and perhaps the line that divides your true tales of the marvellous from story book fiction is so thin, that ordinary persons cannot quite detect it; but never mind, let's have something mild, and I'll undertake to swallow everything you tell me, even if I have to bite it in two first."

"There, now, you're laughing at me before I begin, and you shall not have a strand of a yarn, so you may go to sleep again at once."

Then I had to coax him, and he soon came round. He could not bear to be doubted, much less laughed at.

"Tell me about bringing that little cockle-shell of a yacht from London to Guernsey, that you were speaking about the other day."

"Oh! the 'Dewdrop.' Why, that's no yarn at all."

Then, thought I to myself, here's something really true; and so I afterwards proved it to be.

"The 'Dewdrop' was one of the smallest yachts that ever ventured across the Channel in the month of March. I left London with a fair wind from the west, and got along the London river well enough; but once past the Nore I found it quite lumpy enough to make things very wet and uncomfortable, and after leaving Dover behind I had serious thoughts of putting into Folkestone, or one of the south coast ports, but as I am not one to take a task in hand and then give it up, I shaped my course for Guernsey, making up my mind to give Cape La Hogue a wide berth. There was a high west wind blowing, and a choppy sea rolling the white horses along at a great pace, so that it required some amount of attention to handle a light built twenty-foot yacht. Everything stood as we bowled along, but having no one to help me I felt dreadfully tired and hungry, for I could not leave the tiller to get a proper meal. Two or three hours more and the wind backed a little to the south south-west and blew harder than ever, while, in proportion as the wind rose, so did the sea, so that the poor little 'Dewdrop,' with nearly a head wind, was labouring heavily. How I got through the night I cannot tell, for with cold and hunger I was nearly dead, and what was more, *I was lost.* When I say lost, I could not tell within a score miles where I was. I looked for the Casquet Light, but could not see it. Then I strained my eyes ahead, trying to penetrate the darkness and discern Alderney Light, but in vain. Turning my head to the left I looked out for the lights of Cape La Hogue, but again was disappointed. Where was I? I could not tell, but I fancied I knew where *I should be* in a very short time, for the seas were such as to make it a marvel how such a cockle-shell could float in such a turmoil of black seething water. It was a terrible night, for death rode near me on every crested wave, any one of which breaking aboard would have formed my winding sheet. To make matters worse, towards morning a dense sea fog set in, and I so far gave myself up as to say my prayers at least half a dozen times in as many half hours.

"Although apparently very reluctant to do so, the sun did rise at last, and behold, as the fog melted away, not two miles off, on my starboard beam, was Alderney. I never felt such a thrill of joy in my life as when I saw the breakwaters at the entrance to Braye Harbour, extending their arms as if to receive me into their snug embrace. I was glad to get into smooth water once again, and inside a harbour to boot, for I had never expected to set foot on dry land again. The old hands could scarcely believe that I had crossed the Channel in such a gale; but there I was, and there was the 'Dewdrop' to prove my assertion, therefore they could not doubt it. I pumped her out, and repaired the little craft as well as I could, and on the third day of being in port had eaten everything eatable aboard, and as there was no chance of resuming the voyage yet I had to get some food on 'tick.' This was all very well for a day or two, but after I had been a week in Braye, with no prospect of getting away, the landlord of the tavern from which I obtained my food, told me that as I was a perfect stranger to him he could not afford to keep me any longer on credit. What security could I give him for further food? This was a poser, but the end of it was that I left my whole kit in pawn with him, including even my watch. At length, on the twelfth morning after my arrival the sea became calm enough for me to proceed, and with a west wind I was in Guernsey Harbour four hours after leaving Braye. I think this was the most adventurous voyage I ever made, as it took me sixteen days to make two hundred and fifty miles. I think if the pay was a guinea an hour I should not care about again crossing the Channel during an equinoxial gale, especially to be skipper and crew of such a midge as the 'Dewdrop.'"

"That's what I call a decent little yarn, Alec,—*multum in parvo*—one that might be drawn out into quite a long story, and if it were in the hands of some men they would so spin it out, that the telling would occupy almost as many hours as you were days on the voyage. Nothing like condensing the agony and expanding the joy in a yarn, it makes the listeners in a better mode, and more sociable with each other."

"Sociability," said Alec, "among seafaring men is pretty general. It is usually 'Hail, fellow, well met!' with us, for we endeavour to get all the fun we can out of life, because we know that whenever he gets the chance, Death will have his gibe at us. A sailor must, of necessity, often face death, and therefore his motto is, 'Eat, drink, and be merry, for to-morrow we die'; and death does come to him frequently when least he expects it. I'll tell you an instance of this in which I and some of my relatives were concerned.

"Nine miles from the shore of my native village

there is a most dreadful sand-bank, in the form of the letter U, which at low tide is frequently bare, while at high tide not more than two fathoms of water cover it. It has been a death-trap to many a stout vessel, and at the time I am speakng of had nothing near it in the form of a lighthouse, lightship, or even a buoy to mark its dread presence. At daybreak on a rough November morning the look-out on duty discovered that a small trading schooner was fast on the sands, and after the usual half-hour's excitement in the village the surf boat, containing eleven men, was launched and proceeded to the wreck. There was quite a little party of my family aboard, as beside myself, the crew also contained my father, brother, and two cousins.

"To make a long story short, I will simply say, that after a three hours' exhausting pull we reached the vessel, but were grieved to find that of the crew of six hands, only one was left alive. Our attention was therefore turned to the saving of this poor sailor, who had lashed himself to the bowsprit, where he had sat all through the cold night, and was so benumbed that he could scarcely speak. We shouted to him, and made him understand that if he would cut his lashings, we would when opportunity served, pull the boat under the bowsprit so that as we glided by he might drop in and be saved. His knife was quickly at work, and to show that he was free he held up his hands and moved himself on the bowsprit. We gave him a cheer, and watching our best time, glided in on the crest of a wave to deliver the poor fellow. Alas! in his excitement he jumped too soon, and dropped between the bows of the vessel and our heavy boat. His head was for a second visible on the surface, but before an arm could be stretched out to save him the two vessels came crash together, with his head between them. A gush of blood was all we saw of him, for the next moment we were all in the sea, struggling for our own lives. Our boat had stove its bows in against the ship, which we had approached too closely, in our endeavour to save the poor man.

"I was fortunate enough to secure an oar, and working gradually to leeward of the wreck, with great exertion at length got aboard, where, to my joy, I found my father. The boat still floated bottom upwards, with five men upon the keel, who were constantly lashed by the cold waves, till presently a larger wave than the others broke the hold of two of the men, and washed them into eternity. Gradually in the swirl and foam of the mighty waters the boat beat round to the leeward of the ship, and I then saw that the men on the keel were my two cousins and brother. They could all swim, and seeing that my father and I were ready with ropes, quitted their precarious seat on the keel, and struck out towards the ship. My brother and cousin Phillipe, after a terrible struggle, were drawn aboard, but Gabriel, who could not swim so strongly, presently became exhausted and cried out for a rope. The distance appeared too far to fling it, but with a powerful swing my father threw the coil, the end of which fell a yard short of the swimmer. If I live a thousand years I shall never forget the look of despair upon my cousin's face as he sank back in the water completely exhausted. As his head disappeared his hand, like an eagle's claw, came above the surface of the water and gave one wild clutch at the rope which should have proved his salvation, then it disappeared also, and he was no more.

"Thus, out of eleven men, only four were saved. Incredible as it may seem, these were all of them relatives—my brother, father, cousin, and self—it was quite a family party. We were taken off the wreck in the afternoon by another boat and safely landed. Ducas was a lucky name that day, and so it proved three years after, for my brother was the *only* survivor when his fishing boat was run down, and a crew of eight men perished."

Seeing that we had just had one melancholy recital I thought it best to start something more pleasant, so I handed Alec a large mug of coffee, and said:

"Take a drink, my comrade, and while you are slaking your thirst I will spin you a drinking story."

Then I recounted to him the story of Count Tilly of Brabant, and the Holy Prior. How, during one of Tilly's numerous campaigns, a certain town held out far too long for the general's liking, but at last it was forced to surrender. Tilly had six of the chief men brought before him, and commanded, as the town had laughed at his terms, that they should die, to expiate the rest of the citizens. All kinds of conditions were laid before him to avoid the doom of these unfortunate men, but they were of no avail with him; he was implacable. One, Prior Hirsch, sought him and tried to melt his adamantine heart, and being a man of experience with human foibles, concluded to try the effect of some of the good old wine for which the country is famous, and his own monastery in particular. A huge flagon being introduced, filled with some of the very "A1" of the district, Tilly was induced to try some

"Very good wine indeed," exclaimed the General, "but it is no use your trying to get round me in that way to pardon your burgesses, for I can no more turn from my word than you can empty this goodly flagon at a draught."

"Is the case indeed so hopeless?" said the priest.

"Yes, indeed," said the Count rising. "Drink me the contents of this flagon at a draught, and your citizens are free; else at noon they swing," and with a mocking smile on his lips he was about to stride out of the room, when the priest arrested his steps with,

"One moment, good Count, and I will e'en essay the task."

Then, taking up the flagon, which held *thirteen pints*, he emptied it to the very dregs, and fell back into his townsmen's arms.

Tilly was as good as his word, and released his captives.

"Whew!" whistled Alec; "where's the salt box? Thirteen pints at a draught—thirteen pints! Why, your old priest would make a good second to our maire's cat!"

"What did his cat do?" queried I, innocently.

"Oh, I thought everyone had heard of Curat's cat," premised Alec. "You must know that his cat was growing old and spiteful, so he determined to kill it; but although he tried various means, and got very near accomplishing his end on several occasions the cat would always appear again to trouble him. One evening, as a final effort in assassination, before retiring to bed, he tied a heavy piece of iron round the cat's neck, and dropped it into a water-butt which stood in his garden. Next morning he was down betimes, and standing on the tiptoe both of expectation and of his boots, he peeped over the edge of the tub, when lo! there, on the bottom of the butt sat the cat looking up at him with tears in her eyes, for she was too heavily anchored to climb out."

But I broke in, " Where was the water ? "

" Well, you see," said Alec, " being her only means of escape, *she had swallowed it*, as your priest did the wine, which accounted for her swollen condition. So now, Mr. Thirteen Pints, I think we are about quits."

We were ; Alec scored a point.

CHAPTER XVII.

THE WILL AGAIN—SEARCHING FOR A CLUE TO THE PAPER—BARBE ROUGE'S WILL—A PROBABLE CLUE—HOPES AND DOUBTS—PERPLEXED—A MEMORABLE TRAWL BY MOONLIGHT—A REAL CLUE AT LAST—THE PLACE OF THE SKULL FOUND.

S soon as I was able I went out walking each day, and so rapid was my convalescence that in ten days I was quite myself again. Alec had during my enforced idleness been extra busy, and had made both house and garden look very trim. He had not been able to go far away, for fear I might want him, and thus had spent his time near home.

From joking in the first instance we had now become quite familiar with our new appellations; thus I was Crusoe, and Alec was Monday, that being the day on which I saved him. For the sake of being as near like the hero of Juan Fernandez as possible, I should have liked to call him Friday; in fact, Good Friday, but as he came on the wrong day, Monday had to be his name.

As I write these pages, I can, in fancy, hear his voice shouting to me on the island,

"Crusoe! Crusoe! where are you? Rob—in—son Cru—soe, ahoy!"

Being August, the fruit was ripe and very plentiful; in fact, it seemed a sin to see it hang on the bushes and trees till it dropped upon the ground, simply to serve the purpose of manure. To obviate this we made a whole copper full of jam, and in making it we got into a pretty pickle, both of us being up to our elbows in stickiness, but the jam *was* prime!

Whatever I did, or wherever I went, the paper I had found in the old leathern cup always haunted me. Moreover, when it did not haunt *me*, I haunted *it*; for I took it to various parts of the island, and taking my stand in a certain place, would represent the spot shewn by the skull in the drawing. Then Monday would measure in various directions to see if he could get the measurements correct to certain rocks or tree stumps, to see if they tallied with the paper, but it was no use, nothing would coincide with that faded paper.

We tried the Crevichon, but nothing there agreed; then La Fauconnaire, but could make nothing of that either, so we had again to let the matter rest.

One day, however, it suddenly struck me that as none of the trees on the island were one hundred years old, I might have spared myself the trouble of attempting them when making my calculations and measurements.

By the way, perhaps it would be as well to state

what the precise contents of my document were. Here is a copy:—

"This is the Will of Jean Tussaud, Master Mariner of C—— (sometimes called Barbe Rouge). To the person who is lucky enough to find my treasure house, I herewith declare him to be my heir, and whatsoever he may find shall be his, and for his sole benefit.

"My chief mate, William Trefry, a Cornish man, wished to become my heir before my death, but I could not agree with him on that point, although I left him in possession of the key of my 'petites fées' (little fairies). The key and a valuable knife are all I gave him.

"The bearings of my treasure house are these:—

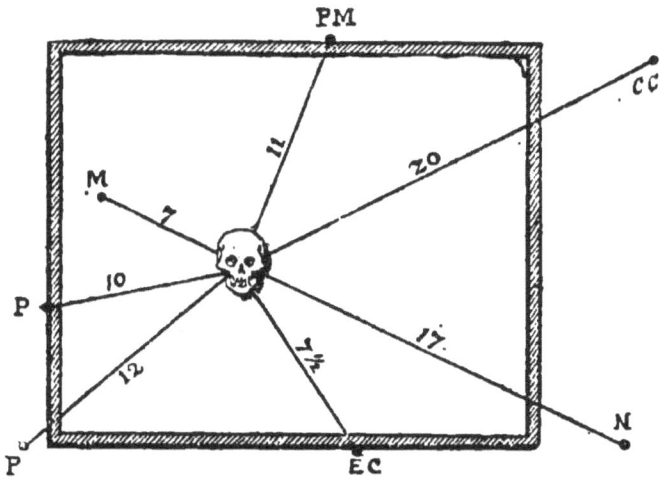

—THE PUZZLING DOCUMENT—

The lucky one will find the following property . . . . . . (Here follows a list of many valuable articles, and winds up with), 'and lastly my pretty box of *petites fées*.'

* * * o * *

"I leave Jethou to-night to join my vessel, which is about to make a voyage to the West Indies, to see what business can be done there. I leave this paper, so that should I never return, the goods I have so industriously and riskily gathered together, may still be of service to someone who may have skill enough to discover their whereabouts.

Signed
"JEAN TUSSAUD (Barbe Rouge),
"Feb. 19, 17—."

Here was a puzzle to which for weeks I could obtain no clue whatever, but one day as I was sitting under the shade of the huge walnut tree overlooking the garden, the idea came into my mind that this kind of tree flourishes for generations, and from the gigantic proportions of this particular tree, it must be a great deal more than a century old.

I found Monday, and asked him how old he thought it would be, and he gave it as his opinion that it was one hundred and fifty years old, if it was a day. Then said I,

"What is the French for walnut tree?"

"Noyer," was his reply, and into my pocket went my hand to bring out the mystic document to see if there was an N on the chart. Joy, there was, and at sight of it my hand trembled violently, and I felt ready to choke with excitement, as I believed I had now a key to the finding of the treasure.

Monday was as excited as myself, all he could exclaim was, "Oh, la, la! Oh, la, la!" which was with him a mark of supreme delight.

We fetched the yard measure, and commenced our survey, as I shrewdly guessed the fine old mulberry tree had something to do with the calculations; if so the distance from the mulberry tree (Murier accounting for the letter M) to the walnut tree would be twenty-four yards; so we measured, but could not make the distance correct, as we made it 26⅔ yards, or just eight feet too much. This quite nonplussed us, and our excitement greatly abated; but we were not yet vanquished, and set our wits to work to discover the meaning of another of the letters from which we could take further measurements.

Being near N (the walnut tree) I walked round the garden wall to the point marked EC, but could there find no landmark at all from which to measure. A century ago something may have stood there, but now it was a bare spot. Here was another rebuff which seemed to upset my theory altogether, and Monday with long visage said,

"Crusoe, you are on the wrong scent, you have 'shaken hands with a shadow.'"

"Wait a bit, Monday. 'A cracked pitcher will hold *some* water,' and although I may be wrong on some of the points, I may find at least *one* correct one presently."

We then walked along to the corner of the wall at the angle of which was the letter P. At this point stood the well.

"What is French for '*well*,' Monday."

"Puit."

"Puit?"

At this I gave a yell of delight.

"Eureka! I believe. Measure away, good comrade; measure away!"

"Where to, noble Crusoe?"

"Ah, where," said I to myself. "Well, measure off twelve yards towards the centre of the garden, and see if it cuts the line between the mulberry tree and the big walnut."

We measured to the wall and climbed over, and continued our measuring, but alas, it went beyond the bee-line between the two trees by about five feet! Wrong again!

Now I began to get angry, as I saw Monday was laughing up his sleeve at me, and I called him *Alec* to shew him I was not in a laughing humour but thoroughly in earnest.

I walked along next inside the wall to about the point on the paper marked P, which appeared to me to be at the window of the house.

"What is window, Alec?"

"Fenetre."

That would not do.

"Now look here, Alec, you are laughing at me again, and I don't like it; laugh some other time, but for the present give me your full attention, and don't be a ninny. It is no joking matter, but one upon which I am very serious and anxious, as I believe there is something attached to this quest which is really worth a little trouble to elucidate."

"And," replied he, still smiling, "when you get to the end of your quest, I believe you will 'shake hands with a shadow' as I told you before. But, Bold Crusoe, I *will* do my best to help you as a good comrade should, so I will bottle up my hilarious mood till you find your treasure, and then I will explode."

"Very well, Monday," I replied. "I trust soon to be able to make you have a perfect earthquake when I shew you Old Barbe Rouge's 'Petites fées.' Fenetre will not do. Now what are we standing near that commences in French with the letter P?"

Monday looked about and quickly said,

"La porte, the door, porche, the porch; how will they do?"

"Capital! now we are surely on the right track."

So again we brought our measuring stick into play, but again the measure was not quite right, but still not far out. We made it nearly eleven yards instead of ten, and although not perfectly correct, it gave me great hope.

With but little trouble we made out the letters PM to be Porte Magasin (door of the store house), and again we were about a yard too much in the measurement. So we left it, and proceeded to the last point, the letters CC.

The point was outside the walls, and the longest distance of all—the figures twenty being written on the line. As in the other instances I asked Monday the names of all kinds of objects to locate the letters CC, but failed in this, except that I presumed C might be Chaumière = Cottage.

Next taking our stand at the point which we supposed the centre of the diagram—the place of the skull—we measured twenty yards towards the cottage, but it fell short of the nearest point of the building by nearly six feet; therefore probably it did not refer to the cottage at all.

We assumed therefore, that a tree or some such

object, to which the letters CC referred, once stood on what was now a pathway joining the cottage.

We paused in our search for the day, resolving on the morrow to try our luck by digging a deep hole in the garden at the spot which we *thought* was the axis of the different radial measurements.

"Begum" followed us about like a district surveyor, and seemed to know something was on foot as well as himself.

Our work of fishing, shooting, and field work seemed quite in the background, and very insignificant compared with my treasure hunt; but Alec seemed to be quite indifferent to it; in fact, I think he had an idea that my fall had slightly shaken my brain, and perhaps addled it. I more than suspected this, for I noticed he kept his eye ever on me, and would scarcely let me out of his sight. Good, faithful fellow!

"What say you to a sail this evening, Crusoe?"

"Just the thing, Monday; it is such a glorious night, and the cool breeze will do us good. What do you say to a drag with the trawl?"

"The very thing; more fish are caught in one night than in two days, so let's set to at once, that is, after a good substantial tea."

The meal being finished, we soon got the trawl and gear aboard the "Anglo-Franc," and away we went in the lovely moonlight, scouring the bottom of the Perchée between the head of Jethou and the tail of Herm. The latter island looked delightful in the pale greenish light of the moon, while Crevichon towering up against the sky, with the moon behind it, caused it to look like a silhouette cut out of black cardboard.

"Who would be stifled up in a town with wealth and its attending cares, in preference to this life of liberty I was leading?" I asked myself, and for answer gave, "While one is young, full of health, and with no encumbrances, a Bohemian life is all very well; but what when a wife and family are dependent on one? That puts a different complexion on the matter, for one can roam no more."

I recollect this night well, for I revelled in its very antithesis to life in England. Everything seemed so strange and quiet; the great black rocks casting their shadows over the phosphorescent waves; the star-studded sky, with the pale round moon, across which a gentle breeze wafted silvery gauze-like clouds; the feeling of motion, the sense of freedom, the love of labour to haul the net, the expectation of what would be our luck, the merry badinage between my comrade and me, our little songs between the hauls, and a score of other things cause me to look back upon this night (and many others) with the thought, "Shall I ever know such happiness again?"

Many persons, yes, most persons, must have recollections of past pure delights that steal across their memories of things which happened long years ago, and cause them to ask themselves the same question, "Shall I ever know such happiness again?"

Why not? It always seems to strike me that when we are supremely happy, we do not realise it at the time; but when the happy time has fled, and has become a memory, we long for its return in vain.

We long in vain for that *particular* pleasure, but there are present joys for us to which at the time we do not give heed enough, or instead of *bemoaning the past* (which has flown) we should live and enjoy the *tangible present*.

From moralising to fishing is a long jump, but we must take the leap and attend to our net again.

After two or three hauls we had almost enough fish, but Alec said, "One more for luck," and he being Skipper afloat, I Commandant ashore, like a good A.B., I obeyed. We had caught several fair soles, but our last haul brought us up two of the largest it has been my lot to capture.

"They are two, but not a pair," remarked Alec.

Neither were they, for when they were measured one was nineteen and a half inches long, and the other exactly twenty-three inches. We christened them Adam and Eve, and like a couple of cannibals declared our intention of eating them for our supper when we got ashore.

As we sailed slowly in against the tide, the question arose who should devour Adam and who Eve; so we agreed to guess the length of the trawl beam between the irons for choice of fish.

I guessed first: "Ten feet."

"There," said Monday, "you have nearly taken my guess out of my mouth, for I was going to say three metres, and that makes it about, let me see, nine feet ten inches."

"How much is a metre?" I asked eagerly.

"Why about thirty-nine inches and a quarter of your measure," was his ready reply.

"Then," I rejoined, bubbling over with excitement. "I've discovered the measurements in the document. Why Old Barbe Rouge was a Frenchman, and of course used French measure,—the metre! Hurrah!" and I made the rocks echo with my excited hurrahs and loud laughter.

Adam and Eve were duly cooked, but they were not half eaten, for either they were too large or our appetites too small by reason of our great excitement; anyhow, Adam would have sufficed for us both, and Eve would have made a capital breakfast for us in the morning. As it was, the mangled remains of the patriarchs remained for our dinner the next day, as breakfast was, under the circumstances of what happened next day, quite out of the question.

As we did not get to bed till four a.m. we were not up till ten; in fact, I slept but little, as dreams of treasure islands, fairy land, and wonderful nuggets of gold persistently kept me tossing about feverishly, till my comrade ran in and wanted to know if he was to dig the treasure up before I was out of bed.

I sprang out of bed and dressed, and in five minutes we were busy with paper and rule.

Hurrah! with metres instead of yards the distances tallied within a few inches, so that near the centre of the garden we had a number of pegs stuck in the mould all round a currant bush, of perhaps three or four years' growth, which had thus accidentally marked the spot that was indicated by a skull on the paper.

Now came Alec's turn for excitement, and he was *intensely* excited. I must say I liked my form of excitement best, for Monday seemed completely off his head, and was gesticulating like a monkey dancing a hornpipe on hot bricks ; he was fairly beside himself. I took mine in a calmer manner, that is, although I was brimful and even bubbling over with it, I did not rave, but kept as cool as possible, and I remember at the time thinking it was due to our different nationalities, the excitable and phlegmatic temperaments predominating in the two individuals and giving character. Probably a stranger looking on would have thought us either a couple of fools or a pair of lunatics.

Off came our jackets, and our sleeves were quickly rolled above our elbows, displaying arms as brown as those of gypsies.

Monday took the pick and I the shovel, and to work we went.

I must not forget to mention that I had told Alec that whatever we found I should consider it my duty to give up to M. Oudin as the real proprietor of the island, and to this he readily assented, mentioning that he at all events could say nothing to my plans, as he was simply my assistant, my Monday.

CHAPTER XVIII.

DIGGING FOR THE TREASURE—A NOONDAY REST—
THE GHASTLY TENANT OF THE TREASURE
HOUSE—WE FIND THE TREASURE—AN ACCOUNT
OF WHAT WE DISCOVERED.

BY noon we had a well-like hole about seven feet deep, and found as we dug that the soil became drier the lower we went, which was unusual, as generally it gets more moist, so that digging at length becomes very arduous.

Although not more than seven feet deep, the earth we had piled all round made the hole look at least ten feet to the bottom, and it had now become very difficult to throw the earth over the edge of the opening above.

It was a hot August day, and the sun poured its almost vertical rays upon us, so that the perspiration broke out at every pore, and bathed us in moisture; but still we toiled on, till, as I say, noon arrived, without our finding any token of treasure trove.

Then said Monday, "What say you now of your quest, Crusoe? Don't you think it's all moonshine, or rather (wiping the perspiration from his brow) sunshine and shadow?

I was fain to confess that it did seem like it, but I asked,

"Will you help me dig to a depth of ten feet from the surface? and if nothing gives indication of what we are in search, I will then give up."

"What, dig down ten feet, and be buried alive in this crumbling grave? Just look at it, it is ready even now to tumble its sides in upon us."

"Well, but," persisted I, "let us shore it up as we go down."

"Very well then," he rejoined, "but I bargain for one hour's rest before we delve further, and here goes for a swim."

Then climbing up our improvised ladder away he went to the beach, whither "Begum" and I quickly followed, and in five minutes we, who had been so lately in a grave, were swimming about in the deliciously cool water, dog and men thoroughly enjoying the exhilarating reaction.

Our bathe being over, we strolled up to the house, and made another attack upon Adam and Eve, and this time finished them; they were delicious. As Monday would have his full sixty minutes' cessation, just as Shylock would have his pound of flesh, we smoked the rest of the time away, and then resumed our labours.

We first took the precaution to shore up the sides of our pit with stout pieces of wreckage and any other wood we could find, for fear of a landslip, which might have resulted in serious if not fatal consequences to us.

Before we had dug ten minutes my spade struck

on something hard and hollow, which quite startled us; but clearing the mould away from the spot, I soon discovered the impediment to be a kind of wooden floor. This we quickly cleared, and found it covered a space about four feet by three. As we lifted the first piece with great expectancy, we found it was oak, about two inches thick, and very little the worse for its long burial, as the surrounding soil was dry.

We looked into the narrow aperture left by the taking out of the oaken plank, but could see nothing, as the depth of our pit made it somewhat dark at the bottom, so I knelt down, and thrust my hand through the opening and felt about. Presently I felt something hard, like a bundle of sticks, and with a tug drew them through the opening, only to drop them the next minute with a cry of horror, for it was a skeleton's hand that came to view in my grasp.

We looked at each other in dismay, as if to say, "How awful! what shall we do now?"

Then we paused, and looked at each other again, till I broke out with,

"There, Alec, your prophecy has come true, I *have* 'shaken hands with a shadow,' or what is very near it—a skeleton. What shall we do next?"

"Had we not better take up the flooring and see if we have come simply upon a grave or what else is beneath us?"

To this I acquiesced. The hole we had dug was about six feet square, to enable both of us to work in it at once; so in this pit or chamber we had plenty of room, and as I have already said, the oak floor we came upon was only four feet by three feet, so that we could stand at the side of the flooring as we removed it piece by piece.

At last we had taken up the nine narrow pieces of oak which formed the floor, and there before us lay the entire skeleton of a man, some remnants of the clothes still covering parts of the frame, and a few locks of yellow hair still adhering to the cranium.

The skeleton was lying face downward, and neither of us liked to turn it over to see if anything could be gathered from an inspection of the front of it, or to ascertain if anything were hidden beneath it; so we both knelt down, and bodily lifted the light but hideous occupant of this awful pit, and placed it in a sitting posture in one corner. As we did so, first a foot and then a leg dropped off at the knee joint, and fell back into the hole, which sent an indescribable thrill of horror through me, and no doubt it acted upon Alec in the same manner.

When we came to look at the awful thing, Alec noticed something glitter at its breast, and reaching forth his hand, attempted to take it to see what it was.

He gave the object a pull, but instead of coming away in his hand, it only had the effect of pulling the ghastly form down upon him, so that the orbless skull came with some force, right into his face. He uttered a cry of dismay, and was about to fly up the ladder, when I arrested his movements by bursting out laughing. The whole thing, although hideous and startling, was rendered ludicrous by the accelerated movements of Alec when the grinning jaws

THE TENANT OF THE TREASURE HOUSE.

snapped right in his face. To save himself from falling into the hole beneath, he clutched the frail form round the body, causing its rags and bones to fall in tatters and pieces on to something below, which gave a metallic ring.

The first shock of his fright being over, for he thought the man had come to life again, we again propped it up in the corner, and examined it closely.

The glittering projection on the breast was the jewelled haft of a dagger, the blade of which was thrust quite through the sternum or breastbone, showing that a most powerful blow had given the poor man, whoever he was, his *quietus*. Death must have been instantaneous, for the position of the blade shewed that it had probably passed quite through the heart.

Another thing also attracted our attention; this was a pair of keys suspended round the neck by a rusty chain. We took possession of both dagger and keys; then placing the bony one in a piece of sail cloth, hoisted him above ground and covered him up.

Down into the hole we went again, almost breathless with excitement, and recommenced our now light task of making further search for whatever might be of value, being fully persuaded that something really worth having now awaited us.

Nor were we wrong in our conjecture, for the first things we came upon were four large dishes of metal, resembling gold; but as they had been rolled up like a scroll by some great force, we did not stop to unroll them to enquire of what metal they really were. Beside them were five or six golden cups of curious work, being beautifully chased, two of them containing jewels in the band of raised work which encircled the stems. Then there were two utensils about a foot high, something in shape between a pitcher and a flagon, which were perfect in form, not a dent being visible in them, their only blemish being the tarnish with which more than a century had marred them, but this could easily be removed.

There were many bundles containing lace, but for the most part this was so mouldy and musty, that it came to pieces with very little pulling, so we threw it aside. Then we came upon quite an armoury of swords, daggers, and pistols; but as most of them were much rusted, we only selected a few of the better preserved ones, and left the rest.

Among those we kept were three pairs of pistols, one pair of which were a marvel of workmanship. The barrels were of silver, and engraved all over with fruit and flowers, while the stocks of ivory were also carved in every part, and were quite perfect, not even discoloured like the wood work in the pit. They were wrapped in soft leather, and enclosed in a velvet case which was in a somewhat discoloured and decayed state, but still in a sufficiently whole form to preserve the pistols intact.

Several swords I kept for decorative purposes, and also some of the huge flintlock pistols.

The bottom of the treasure-hole was filled with bundles of what had once been costly garments of silk, velvet, satin, cloth with gold braid, and wonderfully fine linen; but these were now useless, for time had quite spoiled them. Among these raiments of a bygone age were a number of copes, chasubles, stoles, and such-like ecclesiastic raiment; there was also a beautifully worked mitre, and as these were in good condition we kept them. Their preservation was evidently owing to their being contained in a bullock's hide, which was sewn together apparently by the sinews of the same animal.

Then we came upon a whole pile of sashes, and breeches, and boots, and goodness knows what in the way of wearing apparel, all in a state of dry rot; in fact, they made such a dust that we ascended to *terra firma* for a few minutes to get it out of our throats.

We now appeared to have cleared the place, but what of the "petite fées"? Had we seen them or what were they? To make sure we had secured everything, we cleared the hole completely out, and in doing so luckily saw the end of a box protruding from the side of the treasure chamber. A kind of cave or tunnel had been made for the reception of this chest, and it was a wonder we did not miss seeing it altogether.

No doubt it contained the "petite fées," whatever they were; but to our astonishment it was so heavy we could not move it. We therefore set to work, and cleared away the surrounding earth, and by dint of hard tugging in the confined space, we at length drew it from its hiding place into the centre of the pit. It was securely locked with two huge padlocks.

We concluded we would hoist it out of its bed and examine it at our leisure above ground. To compass this we had to erect a kind of tripod of three long pieces of deal, which had evidently at some time been top-sail yards of some vessel probably wrecked on rocky Jethou. From this we suspended a block and fall, and soon had our iron chest safely above ground.

About this time an unaccountable feeling seized us both; I know not what it was, but it appeared to us that we were doing something wrong, violating the grave of the dead man near us, or something of the kind.

We seemed to feel that the bones should again be buried as quickly as possible, for fear someone should see us at our task. Why this feeling came over us I know not, but it did, so we fastened the rope attached to the block round the waist of the grinning skeleton, and commenced to lower him into his last home again; but he saved us further trouble by breaking in two just above the hips and falling into the bottom of the well-like hole. We quickly covered him with old clothes and hid him from view.

It was a work of some difficulty to get the iron chest to the house, but this we accomplished at last with the donkey's help, and having brought in the other goods, we cleared up for the day, completely tired out.

At nine o'clock, an hour after supper, we retired to bed, each of us fancying we should have our rest stopped by hideous dreams; but we were mistaken, for we slept like the dead in the pit till six o'clock, when we arose much refreshed by our long night's rest.

It was raining fast, and as the drops pattered on the window pane, they seemed like tears for the poor fellow lying unburied in the hole yonder; but we let him lie unburied, as we knew he was past all harm from catarrh or rheumatism, and every other ailment of this world.

We did not go out all day, but devoted our time to examining the great find. The keys (as we suspected) which depended from the neck of the skeleton, belonged to the iron chest; but as they were rusty, we had to clean the wards with oil and ashes, but even then we could not shoot the bolts in the locks, as probably they were rusty. There was but one way left, and that was to raise the lid by force; but even this we did in a gentle manner by filing through the hinges and finishing with a few taps from a heavy hammer.

No wonder the chest was so heavy, for the bottom of it was covered with seventeen leather bags, each containing one hundred Spanish coins, called doubloons, which I believe are worth for the mere intrinsic value of the metal, about ten shillings each, but their monetary value was about twelve shillings and sixpence each. This was something like a find.

At the end of the chest was a portion partitioned off, which contained two drawers, a large and a small one, both of iron, lined with wood. The large one contained three parchment books written in French, the first of which Alec declared was an account of the life of Barbe Rouge, and the other two were log books of his various voyages.*

---

* These books I have since had translated, and find them to be full of "Red Beard's" personal adventures; most of them of such an interesting nature, that coupled with our discovery of

In the right hand or small drawer was a very small gold casket of exquisite workmanship, filled quite full of precious stones in their natural rough state, together with a few cut gems of medium size. I should say altogether they would have just filled a half-pint measure; not that I believe they are ever sold in this manner, as if they were nuts or peas. These then were Tussaud's "petite fées," and pretty ones too.

Of course we put a fabulous price on this part of our treasure; I think in our ignorance we mentioned ten thousand pounds as about their value; but when they were sold in London some months after, in a well-known auction room, they realised but little more than a tithe of this amount.

Next day being fine we carefully filled the hole up again, ramming the earth down with a heavy wooden ram, and finished up by replanting the currant bush, which I believe still lives, or its descendant, to mark the spot where we discovered Jean (Barbe Rouge) Tussaud's treasures.

We presumed at the time that the skeleton we found was that of the mate, William Treffry, mentioned in the document, who had quarrelled with Red Beard as to the property, and that the latter had stabbed him to the heart, afterwards throwing the

---

his treasure, and what I have since learned of him from various sources, I have no doubt the public would be interested in them. Possibly at no very distant period I may publish a book embodying the principal adventures set forth in these manuscripts, as many of the events in the life of Barbe Rouge are of a startling character.

corpse upon the treasure, thus burying his guilt and his goods at the same time. A translation of the books we found corroborated us in this surmise, and accounted for many other things regarding the property which at the time we could not understand.

I may add that among the clothing, we found a number of odds and ends, relics of the eighteenth century, which I still treasure in my home, one room of which forms quite a respectable museum, as since my sojourn in Jethou I have brought many curious things from Holland, France, and Spain, many of which have pleasant stories attached to them.

We found miniature portraits of a Spanish gentleman, and a handsome fresh-coloured young lady with an English name, for their names were painted round the margin; a pair of gloves apparently bloodstained, a case of writing materials, four jewelled rings, a tress of dark brown hair nearly four feet long, an English Bible, two watches with enamelled cases (about the size of small turnips), and several other things which need not be mentioned here, but of which we discovered the history in the parchment books.*

* See Appendix—" Modern Treasures."

CHAPTER XIX.

PREPARING TO LEAVE — A LETTER HOME — WE LENGTHEN AND ENLARGE THE "ANGLO-FRANC" —RE-CHRISTEN HER, "HAPPY RETURN"—LOVE AT FIRST SIGHT—VICTUALLING AND STOWING CARGO—PRETTY JEANETTE—THE LONG VOYAGE —INCIDENTS EN ROUTE—VEGETARIANS, AND THEIR DIET—YARMOUTH REACHED — FRESH-WATER NAVIGATION—MY NATIVE HEATH.

AFTER our discovery my sole thought seemed to be of home. In fact, I was now as ready to leave the island, as I was, eighteen months before to land upon it, and the last fortnight, although it could not have been pleasanter, seemed as if it would never end.

I appeared to go about my work in a mechanical way, and only three things seemed to have much joy for me—my home, parents, and Priscilla.

How should I get home was the next question? I knew my father's vessels were all out to the herring harvest, which begins in August, and ends just before Christmas, so that it was very unlikely he would send for me. Beside this, I wanted to give them a surprise by popping in upon them when they least expected me. To this proceeding, however, there was one great drawback, for, like a true Crusoe, I lacked money, having but a few shillings to call my own. True, I had the Spanish doubloons; but then, again, they were not mine, and if they were they were foreign coins and out of date also, so that no one would have accepted them as current coin.

"What is to be done?" I asked my companion.

"Done! Why there are several ways that I can think of," said Alec, after a pause; "but first and foremost, why not go home in the 'Anglo-Franc?'"

"Monday, you're joking."

"Not at all. We have been out on several rough nights in her, and surely, Norfolk is not such a great way off, that we need fear such a voyage in early September. By your leave I will go with you and act as skipper and pilot, and then, having taken you safely home, will resume my post as King of Jethou. What do you say?"

"But the 'Anglo-Franc' is too small, my good sir."

"Perhaps so; but in a week we can lengthen her, and by adding a couple of strakes to her upper works she will carry a ton more than she does now, if it should be necessary."

"Agreed, Alec. Your hand! Good thought!"

The more I turned it over in my mind the better I liked the project. Why not lengthen and strengthen her at once?

Without delay we would set about it; but to make sure that my father would not send a vessel for me, I would write him a line. As with my former letter, brevity marked my epistle.

"Jethou,
"August 21st, 18—.
"Dear Father,

"All's well. I hope to arrive home about September 10th, and trust to find you all well.

"Your affectionate Son,
"HARRY NILFORD."

Then, launching the boat, I instructed Alec to take the letter to Herm, so that the first boat crossing would take it to the St. Peter Port post office.

I stood and watched him as he neared the little pier at the landing place of Herm, and before he had arrived within two hundred yards of the place, the whole population—men, women, and children—turned out to see him. I am not sure but that the *entire* population was waiting to receive him, for I could only count twelve persons. I think they could not muster more than two or three more, all told, so that his reception was a grand one.

Having instructions from me not to land, he handed the letter up in a cleft stick, and pushing off a boat's length, had a chat with the natives.

"They all spoke at once," said he, "and would not give me time enough to answer their questions, so they got very little information from me. There was one very nice girl there though, that I should like to know, and when I get back from England, I think I shall try and see her parents, for I shall be very lonely all by myself, when you are gone."

Poor fellow! He had fallen in love at first sight with a vengeance. But it is just like we poor men; we are no sooner in possession of enough means to live comfortably upon, than we are sure to want to share it with someone else, providing the someone else is a pretty and loveable woman. Right away from the Creation it has been the same. Adam and Eve set us young fellows an example that it seems will never die out—at least I hope not till we have all found Eves to our liking.

The next ten days we worked very hard, for we lengthened the "Anglo-Franc" nearly five feet amidships, and built her up nearly a foot above her old gunwale, so that by raising the deck or roof of the cuddy forward about fourteen inches, and lengthening it a couple of feet, we had quite a cosy little cabin.

It was wonderful what a remarkable difference these alterations made in her appearance. True, she was only some six inches broader in the beam, but now that she was lengthened amidships she was over twenty feet long, and could stand larger and taller masts. These we soon gave her, so that she now appeared as a half-decked lugger, and, considering our materials and tools, quite a smart little craft.

My occupation of Jethou, according to the agreement, ceased on September 2nd, and as it was now the last day of August, we set about putting everything in order previous to leaving on the 3rd, should the weather prove fine.

It would never do to leave the island without someone in charge; and as we neither of us knew anyone who would act while Alec was away, we were again in a quandary. At last I hit on a bright idea, one that made my comrade's eyes sparkle with delight.

"Did you not say that the pretty damsel of Herm had a father?" I asked.

LENGTHENING THE "ANGLO-FRANC."

"Yes," said Alec, "and a mother too. Would you like them to come over and take charge? Yes? Oh! la! la!!"

Then the simple fellow gambolled about like a young schoolboy, and exclaimed, "Never mind the boat, let me try and swim over."

"Swim, Alec! Don't be a ninny. Do you want to throw your life away in such madness? Go down to the boat directly, and do not act like an ass."

Away he sailed, and soon landed at the little pier, and was quickly surrounded by the inhabitants, who took him towards the cottages out of my sight.

He was gone so long that I became impatient for his return. It almost seemed as if he had forsaken me; but at length I descried him putting off again, and soon he landed, wreathed in smiles, happiness beaming from his eyes. He had settled everything. Father, mother, and daughter were to come over at sunrise on the 3rd, so as to help us off and take final instructions.

The 1st and 2nd of September were occupied in taking in ballast, water, provisions, etc.; in overhauling all the ropes, sails, and gear, and in making a couple of beds of sacking stuffed with the softest hay we could get. Then we had to bake and fish, so as to replenish our stock of food. Fruit had to be gathered, two small kegs filled with water, and finally the treasure and all my little curiosities to be got aboard.

All this took us till long after dark on the 2nd, so that when Graviot, his wife, and daughter landed about five a.m. on the 3rd, we were both fast asleep, so much so indeed that they had difficulty in finding our whereabouts and awakening us. At last, by rattling at the windows we were aroused, and turned out to bid the old couple and their pretty daughter, Marie, welcome to Jethou.

They were very quickly busy, Marie especially, for with Alec's help she soon had the breakfast spread and all ready, and anyone with half an eye could see how matters stood between them. All appeared quite settled.

After breakfast we all walked round the island together, so that I might point out what I required done during the absence of Alec. I introduced them to "Flap," the gull, who seemed to be rather shy of them, as they were the first human beings who had been permitted to interview him since I captured him fifteen months before, except Alec. The goat, " Unicorna," and her companion, or rather son, " Butt," for she had had a son a couple of months after her landing, were next placed under Marie's protection, while my dear old friend, " Eddy," was handed over to Graviot père, with strict injunctions to use him well and not to overload the poor fellow. He seemed to know I was going to leave him, for he thrust his nose into my hand, and made a great fuss of me as I carressed him.

At eleven a.m., all being in readiness, I strode down the well-known pathway towards our little pier for the last time, and it was not without deep regret and dim eyes that I bade farewell to the home in which the past eighteen months of my life had been passed in perfect peace, contentment, and happiness. I could not help a sigh as I thought that this was the last tide I should see rise around Jethou. The last time I should see

> "The busy waters, multitudinous,
> Lip the dry beach, and rippling every pool,
> Embathe the limpets in their swirling cool,
> And plash upon the rocks, returning thus
> To their old haunts with pleasure tremulous."

I loved every rock and tree, and felt loath to part from them, for they were all old friends to me.

I almost forgot to mention that after altering and painting our noble craft, we re-christened her the "Happy Return," trusting that a good name might give us a good voyage, and I am glad to say such proved to be the case.

We calculated the distance from Jethou to Great Yarmouth to be about three hundred and fifty miles, but before our voyage was finished we found we had greatly under-estimated the actual course; but apart from the wish of getting to the journey's end, we had a most enjoyable time of it. We calculated the trip would take us about five days, if the weather were at all favourable, and in this we were not far out. Perhaps a few details of the trip may be of interest to my readers, for a voyage across the channel is not often undertaken in such a small vessel.

As I have stated, we left Jethou about noon on the 3rd, and rounded the southern end of hilly Herm, then we laid our course so as to pass between Alderney and Cape La Hogue, but for fear of rocks gave the cape a rather wide berth, so that about three o'clock we had Alderney a couple of miles off on our weather beam. I was laughing at Alec about his yarn of the "Dewdrop," when an idea occurred to me.

"What do you say to a glass of ale at the tavern you put up at in Braye for those eleven days, eh, Alec?"

"Just the thing. I have not tasted a glass for months."

"Nor I," I replied. "Swing her round," and putting the helm over, we made for Braye Harbour to get a glass of beer. The wind being south-west was somewhat against us, but in an hour we were lying safely in the little harbour, not far from the shore end of the great breakwater, which is nearly a mile in length. We had two glasses of ale each and no more, and having verified Alec's yarn of the "Dewdrop," which was substantially correct, once more embarked, and with a fair wind cut through the water at a smart race. Rounding Cape La Hogue we were fortunate to get the tide in our favour, and by sunrise on the 4th could just make out the entrance to Havre, from which we were some seven or eight miles distant, and passing Fecamp, were abreast of Dieppe at three p.m.

So far we had done remarkably well, and I proposed to Alec, that as I had a little money, we should go ashore and have a civilized dinner and a look round the town; but he took a different view of the matter, and advocated keeping on as long as the wind favoured us, and to this I readily assented, as the wind was now somewhat unsteady.

"Begum" seemed quite to enjoy the fun as well as

ourselves, and made himself quite at home, though I have no doubt he would have thoroughly enjoyed a run ashore, and, as luck would have it, that night he had it.

Some twenty miles further along the coast, that is, beyond Dieppe, we met with our first mishap. The sea hereabout was decidedly choppy, and the wind very puffy, and during one of these puffs we sprung the foremast, which could not have been very strong, as the wind was not at all high. Consulting a chart of the French coast, which we had obtained at Braye, we decided, as it seemed to be setting in for a dirty night, to round in to the mouth of the river Somme and stay the night at St. Valery, so that we could get a new mast stepped early next morning, before proceeding across Channel.

It was lucky we did so, for the wind backed to the westward, raising a lumpy sea, and down came the rain till past midnight, after which the wind lulled and went to south-west again. About two a.m. out came the moon, and quickly chased away the remaining black clouds, after which it was fine again. It did not matter what the weather during the night was, as we were safe in Port St. Valery, from seven p.m. of the 4th, till eleven a.m. on the 5th.

Early in the morning we found a carpenter, who soon rigged us up a new mast, and after a stroll through the busy town to replenish our little stock of eatables, we again pursued our voyage.

From St. Valery to Boulogne is a distance of about forty-five miles, and ere we reached it darkness was closing in, so we took in a reef, as was our wont at night, and lowered the mizzen altogether. This gave us an opportunity of moving along slowly, while one of us slept.

We took it in turns throughout the night to take charge of the "Happy Return," and thus by changing watch every two hours we got a fair amount of sleep. Two hours at a stretch is all very well, but it is not comfortable to be awakened out of a sound sleep in a warm, snug cabin, to take one's turn at the helm; and I soon discovered that three turns of two hours each is not nearly equivalent to a straightaway snooze of six hours, by any means. One has just time to get comfortably off, and then, "Ahoy, there! Larboard watch, turn out!" And then out you come to set for two mortal hours in the wet stern sheets, gaping enough to dislocate your jaw, and longing for the pleasure of dragging your mate out at the expiration of the watch, while you turn into his warm bed with a chuckling "Good-night, mate."

Gaping seems to be very infectious, for on Jethou I have several times noticed that Alec and I, as bed time approached, would sit and gape at each other in a most alarming manner, yet not apparently taking heed of each other's performances, but gradually catching the infection unawares.

On this particular night I gaped so as to be in danger of hitching my upper teeth over the foremast head, in which case I must have swallowed the whole mast, or have signalled to Alec for assistance.

Making the run across from Cape Griznez to Dover is no place for gaping, let alone sleeping; for vessels are so continually passing to and fro that one requires all their wits about them to keep clear of the steamers. These monsters, with their red and green eyes, came looming up so noiselessly in the still night, without the least warning (save these same eyes) of approaching danger, that I almost shuddered as they passed just ahead or astern, to think what might happen if either one of us slept for only a few minutes on his post. Just a crash, a scream, and all would be over, and the great steamer would most likely pass along on her voyage, and no one be the wiser that a couple of lives had been sacrificed to Morpheus.

When morning dawned the dear old chalk cliffs of Dover were looking down upon our little cockle-shell, as she rose upon each glittering wave, and looking up at those gigantic white cliffs, we seemed really to be at home. Here was England at last, and I could not resist the temptation of running into the harbour to once more put foot on my native land. We got in about seven, and had a stroll about the hilly old place, then went to a dining-room and had such a breakfast as my slim purse would afford. We then gave "Begum" (who looked after the vessel while we were away) a run ashore for half an hour, while we trimmed up and made all snug.

At about half-past nine on the 6th we left the harbour in brilliant sunshine, Ramsgate and Margate looking gay with their flags, yachts, bathing machines, white houses, and throngs of holiday makers. The water round the English coast looks hardly clean enough to bathe in after the limpid crystal we had been used to at Jethou. It struck us as looking peculiarly chalky and turbid, but a few days reconciled us to what we shall in future have to put up with.

We kept close in to the North Foreland, to avoid the dreaded Goodwin Sands, as we did not wish to leave the bones of the "Happy Return," with her valuable cargo, upon them.

From the Foreland we took a straight course across the Thames estuary, for what we thought was Walton Naze, but as we had no compass, and were quite out of sight of land, we made a slight error, and about dusk found ourselves close in with the shore. Not knowing where we were, as a fog from the land had come bowling along over the calm sea, we entered a pretty little bay, and dropped anchor for the night.

While we were preparing supper and wondering where we had got to, as there was not a house, church, or other landmark in sight, we felt a bump against our quarter, and immediately after a head appeared above our side, with a "Good evening, mates; I thought as how you might want summat from the town, so I jest put off to ye, seeing ye were strangers like."

"Very good of you indeed, my man. Make fast and come aboard."

Our visitor did not want much inviting, for he rolled in over the side, and squatted down on a locker, as if he had known us all his life. He was a little round-bodied, big-fisted, ruddy man, of about sixty; a thorough water-dog, who, when his tongue was loosened spun yarns and sang us songs till near midnight. He was about the merriest little man I ever met. He had served twenty years in the navy, and was an old wooden frigate man, full to the brim with anecdotes. I thought at the time that it would be worth while for some enterprising editor to send out an expedition to capture him and make him spin yarns to fill up an otherwise uninteresting column of some weekly paper. If I had the space at my command I would recapitulate some of his stories here, but I have not. If I had, my readers would have to take such frequent pinches of salt that they would have a most tantalizing drought upon them, one which would be most difficult to quench.

We obtained information as to our whereabouts, and found that we were anchored in a little bay in the estuary of the Colne, about a mile from the town of Brightlingsea.

On the 7th the sun rose in great splendour, reminding one of the verse:

> "The night is past, and morning, like a queen
> Deck'd in her glittering jewels, stately treads,
> With her own beauty flushing fair the scene,
> The while o'er all her robe of light she spreads."

At six a.m. we were again under weigh (after a good breakfast), and close in with the land, which we hugged right away to Yarmouth, as it was our nearest course.

Speaking of breakfast reminds me of eating, and eating of diet, and diet of health; and this again of my diet on Jethou. Two years ago I used to laugh at vegetarians and call them "pap-eaters," "milk-and-water men," and other pretty names; but while I was in Jethou I had cause to think there was not only *something* in their theory but *much*.

When the weather was too rough for me to fish, I

have often lived for a week or ten days on vegetarian diet, for although I had tinned meat I got tired of it in warm weather, and only ate it occasionally when the days were cold. The pig I killed was more than three-parts thrown away, as I did not properly salt it; so my pork store did not last long.

I used frequently to cut several slices of bread and stroll about the garden and eat my breakfast direct from the bushes, while sometimes I would cook a fish and eat, finishing up with three or four apples or tomatoes with biscuits. Dinner would perhaps consist of a saucepan of potatoes with a fish of some kind, then a rice pudding, or something equally simple, and some cooked fruit eaten with it. I used invariably to stroll through the garden daily and pluck a little of whatever fruit was ripe. I had no meal which corresponded to a tea, but after work took supper, which usually consisted of a scrap of meat or fish, bread and jam, biscuits and fruit. Oatmeal porridge, with fruit and fish, formed my breakfast throughout the winter. It must be remembered that I had a splendid assortment of fruit, and as I ate it freshly gathered I had the full benefit of its medicinal worth, for I had not a day's real sickness while on the island. Excepting the ten days I was laid by with my fall I did not have a single day's real illness. I had raspberries, currants—black, red, and white—tomatoes, apples, pears, walnuts, mulberries, gooseberries, etc., beside wild blackberries; also several vegetables, such as onions, carrots, lettuces, cauliflowers, peas, beans, potatoes, beet, and others.

When I landed on the island I weighed twelve

stone six pounds. When I was weighed at Dover, on my voyage home, I drew the beam at thirteen stone eight pounds; so I was not starved. I was as tough as whit-leather, and as strong as a horse, as we say in Norfolk. With this experience, therefore, I must certainly affirm that a diet of farinaceous food, fruit, vegetables, and fish, will not only give a man good health, but a clear brain, a strong body to perform heavy work, and staying power whenever anything unusual has to be endured or undertaken. More than this, no man can wish for; and even if he is maintained from his youth up on mutton cutlets, or choice rump steaks, he cannot be *more* than healthy, strong, and happy.

Englishmen having for centuries been a meat-eating nation, are naturally reluctant to give up a habit that is almost part and parcel of their nature; but probably if less meat were eaten and more fruit consumed, especially in the warm weather, doctors would be less numerous, and the hospitals be crying out less frequently for increased funds to provide a greater number of beds.

But where are we? Oh, yes, of course, they were Dovercourt lighthouses we have just passed, which seemed to me like two more mile-stones on my voyage home.

The "Happy Return" behaved handsomely, and our cabin was quite dry all the voyage, thanks, perhaps to an extra washboard strake we ran round the bows before starting.

We hoped on the 7th, by evening, to reach Yarmouth, but were doomed to disappointment, as upon night closing in, we were only off Kessingland, a mile or two south of Lowestoft. As we did not want to enter the Bure before daylight, I decided to run into Lowestoft Harbour for the night, which we did, and had a good night's rest. If I had not been so eager to get home I should have passed under the bridge into Lake Lothing, and so through Oulton Broad into the Waveney on my way, but now I was as eager as a schoolboy, and could not bear the loss of even an hour.

On the 8th we slipped out of harbour at dawn, which was about five o'clock, and by seven a.m. crossed Yarmouth Bar, at which my heart thumped so much that I looked round to see if Alec noticed it; probably *if* he heard it he took it for the bump of the paddles on the water, as a tug passed us towing a couple of fishing boats into the offing.

At breakfast time, eight o'clock, we moored in the mouth of the Bure, just alongside the quay by the ancient North Gate, which has looked down upon the muddy old river for the past five centuries, its head held high in the air, as if wishing to avoid the assortment of smells which accompany the floating garbage sailing slowly towards the sea.

How impatient I was for the tide to run up and bear me home to Barton, about twenty miles from our present moorings, and at last it did turn. To give it time to gain strength we waited a full hour, then, spreading our joyous sails, away we sped. I might say we *tried* to rival the express rate, but our actual progress was very parliamentary. We drew only three feet of water, but with a slack tide under us we touched ground several times between North Gate and the One-mile-house, so had to be very careful. From thence onward we had deep water and progressed faster.

It was nearly two o'clock as we lowered sail to pass Acle Bridge, and only about half our journey completed. Stepping the masts, hoisting sail, and having a glass of good Norfolk ale at the little inn alongside the bridge occupied half an hour, but now the river was deeper and the wind fresher, we went bowling along capitally, till taking the turn before reaching St. Benet's Abbey, where we lost the favour of the wind. The flat miles of marsh land looked strange to me after hilly, toilsome Jethou. But now I was nearing home, and knew every tree and fence, every break in the river wall, and every house we passed, and loved them all; greeting them as familiar friends as we glided silently by them.

St. Benet's Abbey passed we turn into the river Ant, and again travel along with a fair wind till bothering old Ludham Bridge bars our progress; so we have again to "down masts" to pass under the single gothic arch, which has been the *ultima Thule* to many a large wherry. Up sail once more, and on we glide up the tortuous narrow stream, till passing quiet, quaint, little Irstead Church, with its two or three attendant cottages, we at last enter Barton Broad.* Now my excitement gives way to another feeling, that of suspense and fear as to how I shall find the old folks at home. Are they well? Who

---

* See Appendix, page 277, "Norfolk Broads and Rivers."

HOME!

can tell what may have taken place during the past six months since my father wrote me, "*All's well.*" I feel a sudden chill as I think of *her* from whom I have been absent for over eighteen months, and reproach myself for not having communicated to her in some way or other. Is *she* well, and is she still *mine?* Then my dear old mother, what of her? With these thoughts crowding through my brain I feel as if I could leap out of the boat and swim the remaining half mile, so slowly does she go through the shallow water.

S-s-s-ssh, bump! and we come to a sudden stop, for my reverie has caused me to neglect my helm, and there we are, fast on a submerged muddy reed bed.

All this inland navigation is new to Alec, and he has been delighted to see how I have handled the craft so far, but I think this *contretemps* rather shakes his faith in my knowledge, till I explain to him the cause of my neglect.

A few hearty pushes astern and we are off again, and as the sun begins to cast its long red rays across the tranquil Broad, with its reedy margin and water-lily nooks, the "Happy Return" glides alongside our little lawn. Joy! I am home again! The wanderer has returned, and the erstwhile Crusoe has once more, like Rob Roy Macgregor, "his foot upon his native heath."

CHAPTER XX.

I SURPRISE THE OLD FOLKS AT HOME—ALL WELL—IS PRISCILLA FALSE—WE MEET—THE MISSING LETTERS—A SNAKE IN THE GRASS—DREAMS OF VENGEANCE.

S I stepped upon the lawn no one was in sight, so treading lightly I walked up to the house, and looked quietly in at the window, peeping cautiously so as not to be seen. To my intense relief the picture I saw within quite assured me that all was well. There sat my jolly old dad and my dear mother, cosily taking their tea, quite unsuspecting who would shortly join them in a cup. They looked very happy; so did a couple of dogs gambolling on the hearthrug, while our old cat sat on a rush hassock close by, looking dreamily at them through her half-closed eyes, when they threatened to knock her off her perch in their play.

I quietly glided in at the side door, and gently opening the parlour door stood in the room before my parents. They both looked round as I made a slight sound; in a moment the quietude was broken. My mother half choked herself with the tea she was drinking, letting fall both cup and saucer on the dogs in her amazement, who scampered away, yelping at their sudden hot bath.

"Mercy me! my boy!" and she fell sobbing in my arms, or rather on my left arm, for my father had taken possession of my right hand with,

"Hang it all, Harry, do you mean to kill us all with fright? Why, my dear boy, I don't know what to say, I feel so glad to see you. However did you get home?" etc., etc.

It was some minutes before their nerves were restored, and I had time to get a few words in edgeways between their greetings. They wanted me to answer a hundred questions, without even pausing to give me a chance to speak; but presently having satisfied them as to the chief points, I thought it high time to fetch in my companion, whom I introduced as "Mr. 'Monday' Ducas, Skipper of the 'Happy Return.'" They quickly made him welcome, taking him to be the Captain of the vessel I had come over in, but remarked aside, that both he and I would look better for a wash and a shave, while possibly a few inches off our hair would make us a little more in accord with the usual mode of dressing hair in these parts. Truly on peeping at ourselves in the glass we did look a couple of wild men or North American trappers.

A tea was then prepared for us to which we did ample justice, but everything seemed so strange. We had not been used to chairs, carpets, window blinds, mutton chops, or even butter, but they soon came back to us as old friends, who had long been absent but not forgotten.

We had a couple of bedrooms assigned to us, also a spare room, into which, on the morrow, I meant to convey our whole cargo; but at present I had neither mentioned our craft or its contents. These things I reserved as a surprise for my dad in the morning.

After we had tidied ourselves I ventured to ask about Priscilla, upon which my father beckoned me to another room, which greatly upset me. Surely nothing was wrong with her; was she ill?

My father noticed my agitation as I asked, "Father, is anything amiss with her? Don't tell me she is ill!"

"No, no, my boy, calm yourself, she is well enough, but——"

"Oh, go on, father, pray do! I can bear whatever you have to say about her except that she has been untrue to me. If she has, I will find the man who has stolen her affection, and——"

"Peace! peace, my son! and listen to me quietly. I believe she is as true a girl as ever lived; but why did you not answer her letters? Twice she wrote to you, but not a line did she receive in reply."

"Letters! I know nothing of any letters from her; all I have received was the solitary letter from you. But tell me what has happened? Why do you look so grave? Tell me, father, and end my suspense."

"Well, as near as I can tell you, Harry, it is this. When you landed on the island it was to be for twelve months only, but at the end of that time I wrote to you stating that young Johnson would wager one hundred pounds that you would be so sick of your exile, that you would not stay another six months on the island upon any consideration. I wrote you, and you accepted the wager, and I find that during the past six months he has been paying his addresses to Priscilla, who——"

"What!" I broke in wildly, "trying to alienate the affections of my betrothed, while he dangled a paltry one hundred pounds before my eyes so as to keep the coast clear, while he laid siege to *my* love. Let me catch sight of the villain, and he shall rue the day he trespassed on my rights. But what does Priscilla say to his protestations of love; surely she does not give him countenance?"

"My boy, you are too hasty," said my father, patting me soothingly on the shoulder; "listen patiently and hear all I have to say, then you can draw your own conclusions.

"Priscilla I know has not given him encouragement, but has returned several presents that he has sent her; but what mortifies her so, is that you have not even deigned to send her a line through all her time of temptation, although she has written twice to you. Johnson's uncle has a large estate in Florida, and being an old man, wants him to go out and help him to manage it. Johnson has consented to go West, and only this week made an offer of marriage to Priscilla asking her to accompany him to Florida as his wife."

"Yes, father, go on."

"Well, I have not much more to say," he resumed; "I know not Priscilla's answer, but this I do know, that if your love for her has changed, she might do worse than accept your rival; but I trust such is not the case."

I could scarcely speak for rage and vexation, to think I had been so befooled by this fellow, and to have given Priscilla cause to think my love for her could possibly change. I would go to her at once. But my father bade me sit down and collect myself, and calmly talk the matter over with him.

"Leave this affair to me, my boy, and join your mother and friend."

I did so, but with an awful feeling of doubt at my heart. In half an hour my father entered the room, and reassured me with a quiet smile and nod, which was of great comfort to me.

Another half hour went by, and then a rustling at the door made me tremble with anticipation and doubt, for something told me it was Priscilla. The handle turned, and as I held out both my hands to greet her, for it was she, she bounded forward with a cry of joy, and fell fainting into my arms.

Here was a *dénoument*. I gently laid her inanimate form on the couch, and was immediately hustled out of the room by the combined force of my mother and our old domestic, Ellen, and not allowed to return for a time, which to my fevered mind seemed an age, but which the clock pronounced to be twenty minutes only.

This time Priscilla came coyly to my arms, and I then knew all was well between us, especially when she turned me round with,

"Dear old Harry! come to the light, you great brown giant, and look me in the face. Ah!" said she, as Alec obligingly held up the lamp that she might get a full view of me, "I can read truth in those bonny brown eyes, but you are a cruel fellow, or why did you not answer my letters? You bad boy!"

"Sit down, Priscilla," and I quietly took her hands in mine, and drew her down beside me on the couch.

"Now, Miss Fortune Teller! what letters do you refer to?"

"Two that I sent you, one in June and the other only five weeks since, at the beginning of August."

"Believe me, Priscilla, I have never received them, and did not know of your writing to me till my father informed me of it, but an hour since. Where did you write them?"

"Here, Harry, in this very room."

"And who posted them, did you do so yourself?"

"No, your father posted the first, and Ellen the other."

"No," interposed my father, "I recollect young Johnson called in directly you left, and seeing the letter in my hand, said he was going up to the village, and would post it for me, so I gave it to him."

Just then Ellen entered with glasses and decanters, and it suddenly struck me to interrogate her on the subject.

"Ellen, do you remember posting a letter to me, about a month ago, that Miss Grant gave you?"

"Yes, sir, very well; at least I went half way to the post, when Mr. Walter Johnson overtook me on his bay horse, and stopped me to ask how Miss Grant was, and seeing the letter in my hand, he offered to drop it in the box for me as he rode by the post office. So as it was such a wet day I let him take it. Did I do wrong?"

"Well, I don't quite know, but never mind, it saved you a drag in the wet, anyhow."

The maid left the room, and then I gave it as my opinion that Walter Johnson *had never posted the letters*, and that to-morrow I would interview him on the subject.

Alec was like a fish out of water at all this "high-bobaree," as he called it; but we now quieted down and spent a very happy evening together, with one or two neighbours, who having heard of my return, called in to pay their compliments.

That night I tossed and turned about feverishly, as my home-coming experience had been so strange, that I could do nothing but think and dream of it.

Walter Johnson was ever before me, and the more I thought of him and his underhand behaviour, the more I seemed to hate him, till at last I felt in quite a frenzy against him. I vowed to myself that in the morning I would see him, and if I could force him to confess his dastardly behaviour in not posting the letters to me, and in making love covertly to my affianced bride, I would thrash him soundly. My only fear was that I should do him some permanent bodily injury if he sneered at me, or in any way tried to ignore my right to put certain questions to him.

Towards morning my plans of vengeance were arrested by slumber, of which I was greatly in need.

CHAPTER XXI.

THE "HAPPY RETURN" INSPECTED—MORE OF MY FATHER'S GHOST—UNPACKING THE TREASURE—SEEK AN INTERVIEW WITH WALTER JOHNSON—TWO LETTERS.

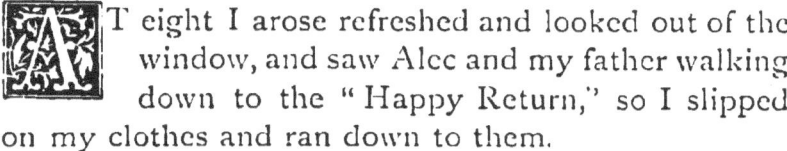T eight I arose refreshed and looked out of the window, and saw Alec and my father walking down to the "Happy Return," so I slipped on my clothes and ran down to them.

Father was amazed to think we had made the voyage in such a craft, and said, "All's well that ends well, my lad; but if you had been caught in a squall in the Channel, with a deeply laden boat like this, what do you think would have become of her crew?"

Then I explained how we had hugged first the French coast and then the English, going into port when we wanted; and how we had been favoured with fair winds and fine weather, which just pleased the old fellow. If anyone wanted an attentive listener let him broach the subject of ships and the sea, and he would at once have my dad as a most appreciative hearer. Shipwrecks and disasters at sea on the East

Coast are, unfortunately, of only too frequent occurrence, and a large volume might be written of the daring deeds that have been performed in connection with them, which have come under my own observation.

By the way, I promised my readers to say more of the vision of my father, which appeared to me in Jethou. Now that I was home I had the opportunity of telling him of this extraordinary occurrence. He was naturally surprised at what I told him, and could only account for it in one way. But let me briefly tell the reader what really occurred to him.

He had been to Yarmouth as usual to business, and in the evening was driving home when, in rounding a sharp turn, his trap was carelessly run into by another vehicle driven by a lad. My father was thrown out, falling upon the shaft of his own trap on his left side. As he was lying in an insensible condition in the roadway, the horse, in trying to rise, fell upon or kicked him in the thigh, breaking his leg. He was conveyed home, and a doctor sent for, who, in a short time, brought him to his senses. Upon examination it was found that his thigh-bone and a rib on his left side were broken. While preparations were being made to set these bones my father conversed eagerly about the nature of his hurts, asking the doctor if they were likely to prove fatal, etc. The doctor told him "No, not necessarily, but he must keep his mind quiet and not worry." Then he told the doctor about me, as it was for my sake he cared most, and it was at this time, viz., half-past eight p.m., that I saw the vision of my father sitting in my room at Jethou. The mysterious appearance was in some way connected with his *will*, but how it was all brought about I must leave to the Psychical Society to fathom.*

About ten in the morning Miss Grant came, and then I proposed that with father's assistance we should get out the whole of the cargo and store it in the spare room. I would not hear of his offer of a couple of men to help, as I wanted nobody but ourselves to know of what our cargo consisted.

Slowly the various cases, bales, and packages were transported across the greensward and safely housed, the heavy iron chest bringing up the rear. This took the united strength of four of us to carry, and when we had put it in the room, I locked the door and proceeded to show my spoil.

First I exhibited the curiosities which we had dredged up, a few stuffed fish and birds, my sketches, curious stones, shells, and seaweed, etc. These were duly admired. Then I brought out the old weapons, and undid the bundles of garments, but being rather musty the effect upon my onlookers was not great ; in fact, my mother gave it as her opinion that they (the costumes) might breed a fever or some foreign disease, and should be buried or burnt. To this I could not consent however till I had had a little more time to look them over and make drawings of them ; not that I ever intended setting up as a theatrical costumier,

---

* I find, on enquiry, that this Society has some *hundreds* of well-authenticated accounts of these occult occurrences, and it really seems that we are often sceptical of these phenomena, without taking the trouble to investigate the cases that come under our immediate notice to discover their truthfulness.

but I have a great love for anything old, which my friends tell me will ultimately become chronic, so that I shall have to be watched when visiting museums and kindred places, for fear of the development of kleptomania.

Expectation ran high as I produced the key of the padlock to unchain the big chest, for we had purchased an old lock at Alderney, from mine host of the inn. The lid was raised, and I produced the three books, but as no one could read them they were put down as evil-smelling things, musty and mysterious.

Next the small golden casket was produced and handed round, amid great exclamations of delight, for I had polished it till it glittered again in the sunlight. The polished gems on the lid and sides found great favour in the sight of mother and Priscilla, who were quite lost in wonder as to where I had obtained it. Presently I opened it, and poured the uncut gems out upon the table, as a sample of Jethou pebbles; but they were not much appreciated, although when held to the light they certainly shewed rich colouring.

"Only fancy walking about on a beach covered with these coloured stones. I should think they look rather pretty when they are wet with sea water and the sun shines on them. But then I suppose when you see them by the *ton*, day after day, you take no notice of them?"

This was Priscilla's idea, and when I told her that they were not so common as to be walked upon or shovelled up by the *ton*, but that they were really and truly diamonds, rubies, sapphires, and emeralds, in their natural uncut state, she would scarcely believe it. Even my mother expressed her incredulity with the remark, "Go along, boy! I suppose we shall not know a turnip from an apple next?"

As my veracity appeared to be at stake I now produced a little pouch of cut, lustrous gems, which at once brought forth quite a different flight of exclamations and queries.

"The ducks! How lovely! How they glitter! See how the sun makes them look as if they were alight! Are they *really* real? Where *did* you get them from? Are they yours?" and a dozen other questions were put to me in as many seconds, but I only laughed and said:

"Now do you believe me?"

The gold dishes, chalices, etc., were also produced, and made a great impression—gold always does.

My good old dad stood by, looking very grave, and gave a very emphatic shake of his head, so I said:

"What do you think of it all?"

Another shake of the head, and then:

"I don't know what to make of it at all, Harry; but if these things are yours, I hope you came by them honestly. Such things are not indigenous to Jethou, you know!"

"Not indigenous to Jethou! Why, Alec will bear me out that they have been indigenous to the island for scores of years, won't you, Alec?"

"It is quite true, Mr. Nilford. These things have belonged to Jethou for a century at least, but I cannot affirm that they are actually the native produce of the island, any more than the contents of these bags."

He thereupon pulled out one of the great leathern

bags and placed in my father's hand, who nearly dropped it, as it weighed over a stone.

When the old gentleman saw the huge silver coins, each more than double the size of a five-shilling piece, he seemed spell-bound.

"What are they? Are *all* the bags full?" he queried.

"Yes, dad; and now if you will all sit down I will tell you the history of my curious cargo."

Then I told them from beginning to end the entire history of Barbe Rouge's hoard, just as it is already known to the reader. I wound up my wonderful recital by calling for pen, ink, and paper, and there and then writing off to M. Oudin, in Paris, giving him a full account of the find, and asking what should be done with the property.

By Priscilla's desire I did not visit the Priory that day, but on the morrow, after lunch, I took my heavy stick and strode up the gravel path and gave a very important rat-a-tat-tat at the great oak door. The servant who answered my summons informed me, much to my disappointment, that both Mr. Johnson and his son had gone to Liverpool the previous day, the former to see the latter off. Something of importance, the servant thought, had caused him to depart two days before the date upon which it was at first intended he should leave Barton. With a glance at my big stick I thought perhaps I had somehow influenced his *hegira*, and such I afterwards found to be the case.

As I was bidding the servant (who did not know me) "good morning" she asked my name, and upon my mentioning that I was Mr. Nilford's son, asked me to wait while she fetched a letter which had been left in case I should call. Mr. Johnson had also left a letter for Miss Grant. This I said I should have much pleasure in delivering, and took them both.

Arrived home I found Priscilla waiting for me in great anxiety, fearing that if Walter Johnson was at home something serious between us might occur. Probably something would have occurred. She seemed greatly upset, and taking me aside, said she had something to impart to me, which I must promise to forgive her for. I consented.

"Then, Harry, I must confess to having written to Walter Johnson yesterday. No, do not look in that terrible manner, for I did it both for your good and his. I simply informed him that you were home and would call upon him to-day, so that if he wished to avoid a violent scene he had better hasten his departure."

I could say nothing to this, as I felt that what she had done had saved a deal of bother. Then I handed her the letter inscribed with her name. To my surprise she would not open it herself, and no amount of persuasion would cause her to. She wished me to open it and read its contents, that I might see all was fair and straightforward. It merely asked forgiveness for the writer for having behaved in such an ungentlemanly manner, and hoping that as all was fair in love and war, she would think of him as one who, having striven for a great prize, had failed. Although defeated, he hoped she would remember him as one not disgraced, etc., etc.

My letter contained a cheque for a hundred pounds, as payment for a wager lost to me, and wishing me every happiness. I ardently wished I could have been near the writer at that instant, and I fancy he would not only have felt most *unhappy*, but that he would have spent a *mauvais quart d'heure*, as our Gallic neighbours say. So much for Johnson, who never troubled us again.

CHAPTER XXII.

M. OUDIN ARRIVES—THE WEDDING DAY—DIVISION OF THE SPOIL—ALEC RETURNS TO JETHOU—WEDDING GIFTS—THE END.

DELAYS being dangerous, it was quickly decided that our wedding should take place on October 15th, my father's birthday. Among the invitations sent out was one to M. Oudin, of Paris, asking him to come and spend a fortnight with us, so that he could kill two birds with one stone, viz., be present at the wedding, and take with him the treasure we had found on his island.

On Michaelmas Day we received an acceptance of the invitation, and on Old Michaelmas Day, which is a time of some note in Norfolk, our visitor arrived.

M. Oudin was greatly pleased with our fresh-water Broads, and as he was fond of angling and shooting he was very interested and happy. We showed him the treasure, of which he made notes in his pocket book, but further he appeared to take little notice of the matter. From his arrival until the wedding day was a period of excitement, and everyone about the place seemed to regard it as a festival; and truly such it was, for every day fun of some kind was afoot, especially in the evening, for then King Misrule held his sway.

M. Oudin spent most of his daylight on the Broad or the adjoining river with Alec, in a small sailing skiff. These two, with rods, gun, and dog ("Begum"), used to bring in quite a good supply of fish and waterfowl, which they captured in the quiet spots a little from the house.

At length the wedding day arrived, and a bright happy day it proved, and everything went "as happy as the wedding bells," and *they* rang merry peals till quite midnight.

Our whole village only contains about three hundred and fifty persons, so everyone who wished came to a meal spread upon long tables on the lawn, and from noon till midnight, dancing, singing, boating, etc., were in full swing. At ten p.m. a huge bonfire was lighted, which had not died out when our people arose the next day.

Before going to the church, M. Oudin requested an audience of Priscilla, father, mother, Alec, and myself, and a red-letter day it turned out to be for us. Briefly, M. Oudin's harangue was this:

"My dear friend Harry, but for your discovery of the articles here before us (the treasure), both by good luck and your great ingenuity, I should not now find myself the possessor of what must certainly be of considerable value. Now, if you have any special wish as to which of the articles you would like to possess, make your choice now, freely and without stint."

I stepped forward and selected some of the old arms, including the silver pistols, the three books, and four bags of doubloons. Then, turning the jewels out of the casket, I asked that this beautiful piece of workmanship might be mine also.

"Is that all, Harry?" said M. Oudin.

"All, and more, sir, than I have really any claim to."

"Good lad; I admire your moderation. Now, friend Alec, and what would you like to take away with you?"

"Well, sir, as the digging was mighty hard work, perhaps you would not mind my taking a bag of the money, for I think it would be of more service to me than anything else, as I can, by changing it, soon make it into such small dimensions as to fold comfortably within the tuck of my pocket book for future use."

"Very well, my lad, your request shall be granted. And you, my dear girl," turning to Priscilla, "what would you like as a memento of my visit, and as a remembrance of your bridegroom's sojourn on my island?"

Priscilla eyed the lace lovingly, and also the gems, but was puzzled in her mind to know how much of one or the other she might select without fear of encroaching on M. Oudin's generosity. M. Oudin quickly came to the rescue with, "Now, my dear, you and Mrs. Nilford divide the lace into three equal heaps, and I will tell you what we will decide upon."

After a time the three heaps were arranged upon the floor, and M. Oudin informed us that he should ask my father to place his foot upon one of the heaps as he (M. Oudin) stood just outside the door. My dad did so, and M. Oudin cried, "For Madam Nilford." Again my father touched a heap with his foot. This time he cried, "For my own dear self." Then bursting into the room he, with extravagant bows and apologies to Priscilla for leaving her out, wound up by gathering up the remaining heap of lace, and placing it at her feet. Then, taking her by the hand, he led her to the table with:

"Now, my dear child, let me pay a penalty for my omission in not calling out your name. With this sweet little hand, which is in another hour to be claimed by our friend here, grasp as many of these rough-skinned little gems as your hand will hold, and they shall be yours."

She grasped, but could only clutch fourteen or fifteen in her hand.

"Ah!" exclaimed our volatile guest, "you see you are not of a grasping nature. Come, Harry, try *your* luck at a grasp."

I took a big grab and succeeded in retaining about forty, so that we had between us much more than half the precious stones. But this was not all, for he continued:

"Now, Harry, I will relieve you of the *whole* of the doubloons, but at the same time I will ask you to put this in your pocket, as a settlement of what you might easily have taken for yourself, had you been anyone but the honest lad you are."

Here he handed me a cheque for a thousand pounds, which I sincerely thanked him for. Then turning to Alec he said:

"Young man, I believe it is your wish to live upon Jethou, and such being the case I shall allow you to retain possession so long as you choose to live there, and in addition to this, in lieu of the bag of doubloons you selected, and which I shall retain, I purpose giving you a sum of fifty pounds per annum, so long as you remain on Jethou."

We all thanked him again and again for his generosity; but he would hear nothing of thanks, as he said the goods belonged to me as much as to him, and in giving away the greater portion he was only acting in a just spirit, in which he declared generosity had no part. "Beside," said he, "I shall leave your hospitable roof with a good slice of the treasure trove, which, although found on my island, was (all but the lace) left by will 'to the lucky discoverer of Barbe Rouge's hoard.' All round, I trust we may say we are satisfied. And now to the church."

In the afternoon I and my bride left for Hastings. Next day M. Oudin, with his heavy packing case of doubloons, bade farewell to my parents to return to Paris, where he had a very large leather business, and was accounted a wealthy man, as his brother had left him his whole fortune.

Alec, in a few days, set out on his return to Jethou, compassing the distance as far as Dover in the "Happy Return," which I had presented to him, but could get no further in her, as a gale from the south-west set in, and further attempt at crossing would have been suicidal. He therefore waited a few days for a stone steamer to take both him and his boat to St. Sampson's Harbour, Guernsey, from which he crossed to his island home.

I may add that as a wedding gift my father presented me with two new fishing smacks, complete with trawl net, herring nets, and other gear. On my part, to Priscilla I handed over Walter Johnson's cheque for a hundred pounds, which was duly honoured by his father.

I think I have now spun my yarn to a finish, and if my readers have been interested in my narrative, I shall, with the sense of conveying pleasure to others, never regret the happy hours I myself spent while enjoying a Crusoe's life in the Channel Islands.

L'ENVOI.

At St. Peter's Church, Guernsey, on New Year's Day, ALEXANDER DUCAS, of Jethou, to JEANETTE GRAVIOT, of Herm.

APPENDIX.

A FEW WORDS ABOUT THE CHANNEL ISLES.

TO say that the Channel Islands are not known to the general public would be to say what is in these modern days of advertising untrue ; but it may be doubted if they are so well known as they really deserve. They might very well be called the "Multum in Parvo Islands," for they contain a very great deal of beauty in a small space ; in fact, it would be very difficult, if not quite impossible, to find another place of the same collective area with such a diversity of natural beauty. Hills, dales, bays, promontories, rocks, trees, lawns, dells, watercourses, and other natural features are here seen in every conceivable variety, and their beauties never pall upon one.

The extent of the islands is roughly as follows :—

Name.	Length Miles.	Breadth. Miles.	Area. Acres.	Population.
Jersey	12½	5 to 7	40,000	65,000
Guernsey	9½	4½	15,500	35,000
Sark	3	1½ at widest	950	600
Alderney	2	½ on average	600	2,000
Herm	1½	½	300	20
Jethou	⅓	¼	50	1 family

Total area, 57,400 acres, or about 90 square miles.
Total population, 102,620.

Everybody appears to agree as to the salubrity of the climate, which is remarkably equable throughout the year. Cool in summer, compared to the continental towns on the same degree of latitude, and much warmer in the winter. As a winter residence it is milder and less changeable than even our favoured Devonshire.

Quite a list of plants might here be appended to shew the degree of mildness experienced in the Channel Islands. Many of them, although of tropical growth, standing out of doors all the winter without taking harm. Dr. Greenhow, of Edinburgh, while staying in Jersey one winter, remarks in a letter to a friend dated January 21st, "I have now on a table before me in full bloom, the following flowers—narcissus, jonquils, stocks, wallflowers, rosemary, myrtle, polyanthus, mignonette, and hyacinths." To these the worthy doctor might have added several more, as the rose, violet, primrose, etc.

Snow is very rare, and usually the night frost is dispelled in a few hours by the warmth of the sun, and the general balminess of the air.

APPENDIX.

For health it is difficult to conceive a spot where a more pure air can be discovered, for beside the fact of each island having the benefit of a sea breeze from whichever quarter the wind may blow, there are no manufactories on the islands to poison the atmosphere with fumes deleterious to health, as in many of our large English towns—even those called country towns. On the score of climate and air, therefore, the Channel Isles will bear comparison with any English county; not only a *favourable* comparison, but one that cannot be rivalled by them, even in the south.

In the matter of hours of sunshine the islands come out a long way ahead of even Devon and Cornwall, as statistics show that for every hundred hours these counties can boast of bright sunshine, the Channel Islands can show nearly one hundred and forty.

The cost of living on the islands is, taken altogether, less than in England; but in the matter of house rent, is somewhat higher. Meat of all kinds is a trifle dearer per pound than in England; but when it is taken into consideration that the Channel Islands' pound is about seventeen and three-quarter ounces of our avoirdupois weight, there is little, if any difference in the prices. Fruit and fish are remarkably good and cheap. The produce in the markets of Guernsey and Jersey are an unusual sight to visitors, for the fruit is placed for customers' inspection just as it is gathered, so that the plums, grapes, etc., retain their bloom and look a perfect picture. The fish is brought in straight from the sea, still retaining its iridescent hues, and there is no need to enquire further if they are fresh, as they, to put it metaphorically, speak for themselves. Coal has to be imported from England and Belgium, and is therefore somewhat expensive; but it must be remembered that the climate, being so mild, does not necessitate so much being consumed.

Wines and spirits are now, since the imposition of a Duty only a trifle lower in price than in England, but perhaps of inferior quality. Tobacco and cigars are ridiculously cheap, but not always nasty, because of their cheapness. Anyone content to smoke a cigar of fair quality may do so at a price about fifty per cent. less than in England; but if he is fastidious in his taste, and requires something superior, such as a genuine Havanna, he will look for it in vain. Strangely enough he can be obliged at most cigar dealers with Havanna cigars at Havanna prices, but as the Customs pass very few of the genuine cigars, it is a mystery where they all come from. Yet they say smuggling is a thing of the past! Or do the gentle tradesmen, to discourage smuggling, manufacture their own *Havannas?* Good tobacco, shag and bird's-eye, may be had at eighteen pence per pound.

There are several routes to the Islands, the chief being in connection with our large railways, and are undoubtedly the quickest and most comfortable. Those fond of the sea may make the trip from London by steamer any Saturday throughout the summer, a distance of nearly three hundred miles for about a sovereign for the return journey. Another route, for Cornish people, is from Falmouth. From Plymouth west of England residents can take passage by a comfortable steamer any Friday, which covers the distance to Jersey in about ten hours. The route from Southampton is a favourite one, as although not the shortest sea route, it is within such a small railway journey of London as to be reached in about a couple of hours. The distance by water by this route (one hundred and fifteen miles) does not apparently compare favourably with the eighty miles from Weymouth to Guernsey; but it must be remembered that the trip down the Southampton Water and along the shore of the Isle of Wight, till the Needles are passed, is all smooth sailing. The actual distance on the open sea is therefore not very much further than by the Weymouth route.

The steamers which, by the by, carry the mails to the Channel Isles, are very large and powerfully-built vessels, fitted with every modern appliance for the comfort of travellers. The London and South-Western Railway may also be congratulated on having just the right men for captains of their vessels. Men who, beside being capable navigators, are also alive to the comfort of those who are temporarily in their charge. Still, another route is by the Great Western Railway from Weymouth.

I would add a final word to those who are about to hie *abroad* for a genial climate, for beautiful scenery, or to see something not to be seen elsewhere. Have they thought of the Channel Islands? If not, let them try a month there, and if they are not pleased, there is the French coast only twenty miles away. Should they not have gained all they expected in a visit, they will at least have acquired one thing, and that is a month's health.

Modern Treasure.

Although the spoil we discovered on Jethou was worth a very considerable amount, yet it appears quite insignificant beside some modern treasure which has been either sought after or found, as the following items, clipt from the London newspapers for July, 1891, will shew :—

"A Dalziel's telegram from Berlin reports that a large treasure of gold coins, of the size of twenty-mark pieces, has been found at Beuthen, in Silesia. Part of them bear the date 1508. There are reported to be a million coins in all."

"His Majesty King James II. of England certainly gave a good deal of trouble during his lifetime, and is now proving a nuisance indirectly in a very extraordinary way, one hundred and ninety years after his death. According to an ancient local legend, James, who died at Saint Germain-en-Laye, hid away somewhere in the neighbourhood of the monastery of Triel, the royal crown of England, the sceptre, and other baubles of a total value of some £2,000,000. For more than forty years past the owners of the estate on which are the ruins of the monastery, have sought for the regalia by digging long trenches in all directions, always starting from the building itself. This having become a serious danger to the neighbouring village, the mayor is taking steps to prevent any further delving by the seekers after hidden treasure."

Jarrold and Sons, Printers, Norwich, Yarmouth, and London.

Selections from Jarrolds' New Books.

BOOKS OF ADVENTURE FOR BOYS.
Crown 8vo, Cloth. 3/6 each.

The Story Hunter. By E. R. SUFFLING, Author of "*Afloat in a Gipsy Van,*" "*Jethou, or Crusoe Life in the Channel Islands.*" Illustrated by PAUL HARDY. 2nd Edition.

A volume so varied in its contents as to please many tastes. Hypnotism is the weapon which the Story Hunter uses to bring down his quarry—uses, too, with such effect that he is able to present to the reader a collection of thrilling narratives of the most heterogeneous character.

"The stories themselves purport to be a collection formed by a gentleman who lives in a caravan, journeys about the country, hypnotises likely subjects, and obtains from them, when in that state, tales of remarkable events that have happened to them. These tales are all striking, and quite out of the ordinary line. There is certainly no lack of imagination in these tales."—*The Standard.*

"The stories are highly imaginative, and form a very interesting book."—*Essex Herald.*

"There is splendid stuff in this book for boys. Mr. Suffling knows how to thrill and mystify."—*Cork Examiner.*

"They are certain to delight any boys who have a liking for the supernatural."—*Scotsman.*

"There are plenty of entertaining short tales in 'The Story Hunter.'"—*Graphic.*

"A very entertaining volume."—*Daily Chronicle.*

"A volume consisting of some ten stories, not one of which is weak or ineffective. We can recommend the book as being a capital volume of literature."—*Observer.*

"'The Story Hunter' is an absorbing collection of tales, told by a gentleman who is in the habit of travelling about the country in a caravan."—*Elizabethan.*

"The stories are well told, and will be acceptable to young people."—*Morning Post.*

"There is certainly no lack of imagination in these tales, and we predict that few who start reading them will have done with the book until they reach the end of it."—*Devon and Exeter Gazette.*

"Curious and fascinating are several of the stories. The book is nicely illustrated, and would form a capital prize or present."—*Schoolmaster.*

"Nine or ten quaint tales, in which the supernatural plays a very important part."—*The Gentlewoman.*

"The tales are well told, and full of interest."—*School Guardian.*

"Mr. Suffling knows parts of England well, and places his stories in scenes that will make them enjoyable to readers of all ages."—*Spectator.*

London: Jarrold and Sons, 10 and 11, Warwick Lane, E.C.
Of all Booksellers and at the Bookstalls.

Selections from Jarrolds' New Books.

NEW BOOK OF ADVENTURE FOR BOYS.

Crown 8vo, Illustrated, Handsomely Bound, Cloth, Olivine Edges. Price 3s. 6d. (Postage 4½d.)

Afloat in a Gipsy Van.

By E. R. SUFFLING, Author of "*Jethou; or, Crusoe Life in the Channel Islands*," &c. With beautiful Illustrations by PAUL HARDY. 3s. 6d.

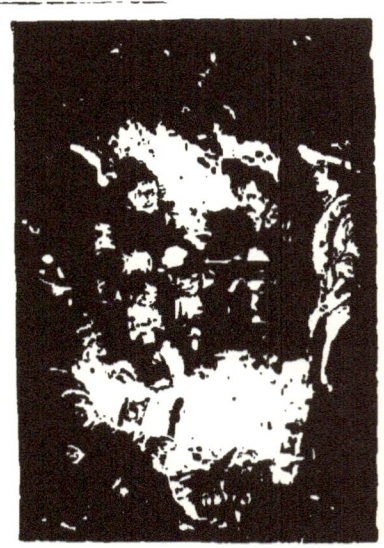

Being the wanderings and adventures of three lads under the care of one, "Uncle Rue." It shows how a Gipsy Van is made to float safely down the East Coast and across the North Sea to Holland, and recounts the experience of the quartette both on sea and land.

"A capital book for boys."—*Daily Chronicle.*

"It is ingenious, bright, and well-written, and will tend to develop the resourcefulness of the boys who read it."—*Independent.*

"About the most novel and ingenious book for boys we have seen for some time."—*Aberdeen Free Press.*

"Cannot fail to prove exceptionally interesting."—*Christian World.*

"Will prove of absorbing interest to those lads who delight in tales of perseverance and pluck, and all that can be accomplished by these qualities. The volume is cleverly illustrated by Paul Hardy."—*Belfast News Letter.*

"It is a lively and well-written story."—*Bradford Observer.*

"Every boy's eye will brighten on seeing 'Afloat in a Gipsy Van.' The story is strongly original in conception, and is treated with a vigour becoming a stirring recital of adventure."—*Dundee Advertiser.*

"It has a lively plot, which is always on the move, and adventures enough to fill forth a dozen books, while the interest is always bright and changing."—*Scotsman.*

"Mr. Suffling's yarn, which inculcates the need of courage, perseverance, and obedience for the attainment of a desired end, will certainly delight and interest a very large audience."—*Christian Age.*

"We are delighted with the whole narrative, and predict for it a great success as a prize book."—*Teachers' Aid.*

"It is very well put together and written."—*Literary World.*

"It is a stirring narrative throughout, and youthful readers will find in its pages as much of danger, strange adventures, and singular situations as the most exacting of them can demand. And with all this, the limits of the possible and probable are not exceeded."—*Leeds Mercury.*

London: Jarrold and Sons, 10 and 11, Warwick Lane, E.C.
Of all Booksellers and at the Bookstalls.

Selections from Jarrolds' New Books.

MR. HUTCHESON'S NEW BOOK FOR BOYS AND GIRLS.
Crown 8vo, Cloth elegant. 3/6.

Bob Strong's Holidays;
OR, ADRIFT IN THE CHANNEL.
By the Author of "*Afloat at Last,*" "*The Wreck of the Nancy Bell,*" &c. With Six Illustrations by JOHN B. GREENE. 2nd Edition.

A bright, brisk, breezy book, breathing out healthy ozone from every page; full of incident and adventure, such as will be liked and loved by every boy and girl reader.

"Mr. Hutcheson, being so well-known as a favourite writer for boys, the volume will, we are sure, prove very popular. The book deals with a cruise in the channel, and the adventures which happened to Bob Strong during the cruise."—*Devon and Exeter Gazette.*

"'Bob Strong's Holidays; or, Adrift in the Channel,' by John C. Hutcheson, is the story of the deadly peril of two youths of resources, who were cast adrift at sea in an open boat."—*Daily News.*

"'Bob Strong's Holiday' is a perfect story for boys. It shows us how Bob Strong's holiday is of a particularly adventurous order. He makes the acquaintance in the train, on the way home from school, of Dick Allsop, who has run away from home and the tyranny of a cruel step-father; and at Portsmouth, whither the boys are bound, they fall in with Captain Dresser, and the adventures, which are the result of the friendship which springs up between the three, are of a very interesting character, and are admirably related."—*Norfolk Chronicle.*

"This healthy tale for boys, from the pen of Mr. Hutcheson, comes very opportunely. The plot is extremely simple, and yet Mr. Hutcheson keeps up the interest of the reader in Bob Strong in a wonderful manner. The book is attractive in appearance, and is a good presentation work for boys."—*Cambridge Daily News.*

"It is a fine tale of the sea, full of thrilling situations, accompanied with a host of illustrations by Mr. John B. Greene."—*Book and News Trades' Gazette.*

"Another sterling sea story, that may safely be placed in any boy's hands. As a whole, these are the most attractively-written and best illustrated volumes we have seen this season."—*Board Teacher.*

"From Messrs. Jarrold and Sons, London, comes a tale for young readers, written by Mr. John C. Hutcheson, and illustrated by J. B. Greene. It is a spirited and lively tale of the adventures of a lad who got adrift at sea, although this is only the culmination of his 'larks,' and might have been lost if it hadn't been for the fisher folk. Its title is 'Bob Strong's Holidays,' and it is a capital book for a boy."—*The Scotsman.*

London: Jarrold and Sons, 10 and 11, Warwick Lane, E.C.
Of all Booksellers and at the Bookstalls.

Selections from Jarrolds' New Books.

BEAUTIFUL JOE.
THE AUTOBIOGRAPHY OF A DOG.
BY MARSHALL SAUNDERS.

42nd Thousand.   Illustrated, 3/- (Post 4½d.)   Gilt Edges, 3/6.

The Countess of Aberdeen writes of the Canadian edition of "Beautiful Joe": "I am sure that all lovers of animals will welcome this book with eagerness as being eminently calculated to spread that knowledge and thought for dumb beasts which will lead to their humane treatment."

"The narrative is admirably conveyed and interesting from every point of view. If we had our wish and our way, the book should be in every school and in every house."—*The World.*

"The book is charmingly got up, and would make an excellent school-prize."—*British Weekly.*

"It is a capital story, and is certain to be popular among all lovers of animals."—*Sheffield Daily Telegraph.*

"For Sunday-school libraries and for reading alike in families, it is a most appropriate volume, sure to draw out the sympathies of young readers to their four-footed companions, and to teach them valuable lessons as to the right and kind treatment of dumb creatures."—*The Freeman.*

London: Jarrold and Sons, 10 and 11, Warwick Lane, E.C.
Of all Booksellers and at the Bookstalls.

Selections from Jarrolds' New Books.

BOOKS OF ADVENTURE FOR BOYS.
Crown 8vo, Cloth. 3/6 each.

The Boy Skipper: A TRUE STORY OF THE SEA. By W. C. METCALFE, Author of "*Nailing the Colours*," &c. Illustrated by ENOCH WARD. 2nd Edition.

The hero of this book is a living person—William Shotton, of Sunderland. The story, therefore, has the advantage of being true, and receives, in confirmation of its truth, the imprimatur of an authorised dedication to *Lloyd's*. Moreover, it is replete with manly thought and sound principle, and boys of all ages will be the better for hearing how the "Boy Skipper" navigated the good ship *Trafalgar* from Java to Melbourne, under exceptionally trying and discouraging circumstances.

"We have rarely read a more admirable boy's story than this."—*Schoolmaster*.

"In 'The Boy Skipper' Mr. Metcalfe narrates the real adventures of William Shotton, who received a medal and a handsome gratuity from the members of Lloyd's for saving the ship *Trafalgar*, with its valuable cargo."—*The Times*.

"No more inspiring story of heroism for boys could be found."—*Daily News*.

"The volume will be acceptable as the true story, well told of a British lad's pluck, energy, and resource."—*Morning Post*.

"We cannot imagine a more pleasing and inspiring gift book for a boy."—*Whitehall Review*.

"A skilfully-woven piece of biography. One that it would be well to put into every lad's hands."—*Truth*.

"It is a true story of the life and adventures of a Sunderland sailor boy."—*Glasgow Herald*.

"Mr. W. C. Metcalfe has spared no pains to make the heroism of Mr. Shotton as realistic as possible."—*Newcastle Daily Leader*.

"Boys ought to take eagerly to 'The Boy Skipper.'"—*Birmingham Daily Gazette*.

"'The Boy Skipper' has the additional and superlative merit of being true. No fitter exemplification of a high conception of duty could have occupied Mr. Metcalfe's pen."—*Christian Age*.

"A fascinating story of fact, which all readers will enjoy."—*Fairplay*.

"A book of entrancing interest to boys, and with much to engage the attention of those of older growth."—*Leeas Mercury*.

"A capital sea story for boys, having the merit of being founded on fact."—*Liverpool Daily Post*.

London: Jarrold and Sons, 10 and 11, Warwick Lane, E.C.
Of all Booksellers and at the Bookstalls.

Selections from Jarrolds' New Books.

BOOKS OF ADVENTURE FOR BOYS.
Crown 8vo, Cloth. 3/6 each.

Far from Home: THE FIGHTS AND ADVENTURES OF A RUNAWAY. By ROBERT OVERTON, Author of "*Lights Out*," "*King's Pardon*," "*After School*," &c. Illustrated by ENOCH WARD. 2nd Edition.

A story of adventure, wherein the strange and perilous experiences of a runaway, his encounters and escapes (especially among the pirates of Kermadec), the companions he falls in with, and the lands he visits, are fully enumerated and disclosed.

"'Far from Home' is really a capital story. Mr. Overton shows exceptional ingenuity and freshness."—*The Times.*

"This new volume abounds in stirring adventure, and is bright and wholesome in tone."—*Morning Leader.*

"There could be no better book for a boy who likes a rousing, thundering, go-head story."—*Scotsman.*

"Beautifully got up and nicely illustrated, 'Far from Home' is a most suitable and delightful book for boys."—*Aberdeen Free Press.*

"Boys cannot do better than consult Mr. Overton's always brisk and breezy narrative."—*Daily Telegraph.*

"'Far from Home' is by that delightful writer of school yarns, Robert Overton, and records with actuality and vividness the fights and adventures of a runaway."—*Christian World.*

"This is a delightful book of stirring adventure."—*Manchester Courier.*

"Surely it is enough praise to say the story is worthy of an equally welcome reception from boy readers to this author's favourite stories."—*Preston Guardian.*

"It is a fascinating story of adventure in two hemispheres."—*Pall Mall Gazette.*

"It teems with exciting incidents, including some collisions with bushrangers."—*Weekly Sun.*

"In 'Far from Home,' another youth is added to the great army of runaways. Boys with a tendency that way had better study this book carefully before they run away to sea, and boys who have no such intentions will find it equally good reading."—*Westminster Gazette.*

"Wholesome and interesting."—*The Guardian.*

"A due meed of recognition certainly awaits the very excellent story by Mr. Overton. The boy who cannot find delight herein deserves to be clad in bloomers."—*Truth.*

"The book is of good, breezy, moral tone. We anticipate that Mr. Overton's latest venture will become a favourite boy's book."—*Schoolmaster.*

London: Jarrold and Sons, 10 and 11, Warwick Lane, E.C.
Of all Booksellers and at the Bookstalls.

www.ingramcontent.com/pod-product-compliance
Lightning Source LLC
Chambersburg PA
CBHW031932230426
43672CB00010B/1905